STUDY MANUAL

THE PROPHETIC ENDGAME

HARRISON HOUSE AND DESTINY IMAGE BOOKS BY JOSEPH Z

The Prophetic Endgame: The Book of Revelation, the Return of Jesus, and the Battle for Eternity

The Prophetic Endgame Study Manual

Servants of Fire: Secrets of the Unseen War & Angels Fighting for You

Breaking Hell's Economy: Your Guide to Last-Days Supernatural Provision

Breaking Hell's Economy Study Manual

The Spirit of Elijah: Expose the Truth, Embrace God's Power, Break the Antichrist Spirit

The Spirit of Elijah Study Manual

Punishing the Darkness: Spiritual Warfare That Works

Punishing the Darkness Study Manual

Demystifying the Prophetic: Understanding the Voice of God for the Coming Days of Fire

Demystifying the Prophetic Study Manual

The Secret to the Life of John: A Revelation for a Supernaturally Long-Lasting Life

A Prophet's Reward: Partnering with the Prophetic for Your Faith, Favor, and Financial Miracles

Weaponizing Your Faith: Supernaturally Equipped to Receive Your Breakthrough

The Origin of the Cosmic Battle

Jesus and the Kingmakers

STUDY MANUAL

THE PROPHETIC ENDGAME

THE BOOK OF REVELATION, THE RETURN OF JESUS, AND THE BATTLE FOR ETERNITY

JOSEPH Z

All emphasis within Scripture quotations is the author's own.

Published by Harrison House Publishers

Shippensburg, PA 17257

ISBN 13 TP: 9781667514758

ISBN 13 eBook: 9781667514765

For Worldwide Distribution, Printed in the U.S.A.

1 2 3 4 5 6 7 8 / 30 29 28 27 26

CONTENTS

LETTER FROM JOSEPH Z

Dear Reader,

When I set out to write *The Prophetic Endgame* book and this manual, my deepest desire was to build anticipation for the glorious future that awaits every believer—not just the immediate "end times" often discussed, but what comes *after* the Great White Throne Judgment, as we step into eternity with God Almighty. This long-term epoch, chosen and endured by God on our behalf, is filled with a purpose not yet fully revealed in Scripture, which is what captivated my heart and ignited this journey.

Throughout history, God has operated by revealing His secrets to His servants, the prophets, as seen in Amos 3:7. This is the very pattern we find in the book of Revelation, where Jesus unveiled the divine plan to John. While Deuteronomy 29:29 speaks of the secret things belonging to the Lord, Proverbs 25:2 encourages us, as "kings," to search out the "concealed matters." I believe there is an even greater pursuit for New Testament believers. Through the Holy Spirit, we have revelatory access to the mysteries of God and a relationship that can lead to insights regarding His covenant, even into eternity future. As we renew our minds with Scripture, His secrets will be with us, though He ultimately reveals them as He wishes.

The book of Revelation is not a historical account; it is prophecy (*see* Revelation 1:3). It shows us what *has been seen* (the vision of Christ in chapter 1), what *is* (the letters to the seven churches), and the events *which will take place after this* (chapters 4–22). Its primary focus is the approaching kingdom without end and the return of Jesus, the warrior King, who will take authority over all the kingdoms of the earth.

As we are plunged into the last of the last days, the conflict between life and death, truth and lies, clarity and chaos, is only gaining momentum. Events rising around the earth are merely an extension of the ancient mischief that began with Lucifer's rebellion. We will examine the true nature of this rebellion and the endgame of the dark forces erroneously attempting to place that mutinous fallen angel on God's throne—the driving spirit behind the Antichrist's eventual rise.

But there is a glorious theme that unfolds throughout the ages: God wants His family with Him and has gone to great lengths to make it a reality. Consider what was required for Jesus, the Word, to become flesh. God could not simply undo Adam's fall, which tragically gave dominion over the earth to Satan through a legal technicality. Instead, like a master chess player, God worked within His own rules, weaving the plan of redemption into the fabric of the world. He chose the long road to defeat darkness at their own game because of His eternal desire for His children.

This manual is the result of searching the Scriptures to grasp better where we are heading. To understand our eternal future, we must examine the beginning and even what may have been taking place in eternity past. It is the pinnacle of hope to know that our Great God loves to conceal Himself so that we may draw out His truth.

You will find that every page of this work is woven with detailed information from the Word of God. It is my sincere prayer that it strengthens your faith, sets a course in your heart to uncover God's concealed things in His Word, and fills you with hope as you discover His grand plan for humanity, made available only through our Lord and Savior, Jesus Christ.

> Wisdom is the principal thing; therefore get wisdom....
>
> —Proverbs 4:7

In all your getting, may you gain understanding of what was, and is, and is to come.

Joseph Z

MANUAL INSTRUCTIONS

The Prophetic Endgame Study Manual was created to help individuals deepen their understanding while reading *The Prophetic Endgame*. This manual is a companion to the reading book, with each section featuring questions and additional information for reflection. The answers are in the section you read in the book, but there's room for your thoughts and answers. The Focus Points and Personal Reflections are opportunities for you to delve deeper and seek the Lord for answers, fostering personal growth. Some questions may require your honesty; in moments of uncertainty, let the Holy Spirit guide you. May God bless you on your journey through *The Prophetic Endgame* book and study manual.

SECTION ONE

To Understand the End, We Must Go to the Beginning...

CHAPTER ONE

JESUS, AVENGER OF BLOOD

SCRIPTURES

1. **Revelation 1:7-8**—*Behold, He is coming with clouds, and every eye will see Him, even they who pierced Him. And all the tribes of the earth will mourn because of Him. Even so, Amen. 8 "I am the Alpha and the Omega, the Beginning and the End," says the Lord, "who is and who was and who is to come, the Almighty."*

2. **Revelation 6:15-16**—*And the kings of the earth, the great men, the rich men, the commanders, the mighty men, every slave and every free man, hid themselves in the caves and in the rocks of the mountains, 16 and said to the mountains and rocks, "Fall on us and hide us from the face of Him who sits on the throne and from the wrath of the Lamb!"*

3. **Exodus 33:20**—*But He said, "You cannot see My face; for no man shall see Me, and live."*

4. **Daniel 7:13-14**—*I was watching in the night visions, and behold, One like the Son of Man, coming with the clouds of heaven! He came to the Ancient of Days, and they brought Him near before Him. 14 Then to Him was given dominion and glory and a kingdom, that all peoples, nations, and languages should serve Him. His dominion is an everlasting dominion, which shall not pass away, and His kingdom the one which shall not be destroyed.*

5. **Matthew 24:30**—*Then the sign of the Son of Man will appear in heaven, and then all the tribes of the earth will mourn, and they will see the Son of Man coming on the clouds of heaven with power and great glory.*

6. **Matthew 26:64**—*Jesus said to him, "It is as you said. Nevertheless, I say to you, hereafter you will see the Son of Man sitting at the right hand of the Power, and coming on the clouds of heaven."*

7. **Zechariah 12:10-11**—*And I will pour on the house of David and on the inhabitants of Jerusalem the Spirit of grace and supplication; then they will look on Me whom they pierced. Yes, they will mourn for Him as one mourns for his only son, and grieve for Him as one grieves for a firstborn.* [11] *In that day there shall be a great mourning in Jerusalem, like the mourning at Hadad Rimmon in the plain of Megiddo.*

8. **Isaiah 63:1-6**— *Who is this who comes from Edom, with dyed garments from Bozrah, this One who is glorious in His apparel, traveling in the greatness of His strength?—"I who speak in righteousness, mighty to save."* [2] ***Why is Your apparel red, and Your garments like one who treads in the winepress?*** [3] ***"I have trodden the winepress alone****, and from the peoples no one was with Me. For I have trodden them in My anger, and trampled them in My fury;* ***their blood is sprinkled upon My garments****, and I have stained all My robes.* [4] *For the day of vengeance is in My heart, and the year of My redeemed has come.* [5] *I looked, but there was no one to help, and I wondered that there was no one to uphold; therefore My own arm brought salvation for Me; and My own fury, it sustained Me.* [6] *I have trodden down the peoples in My anger, made them drunk in My fury, and brought down their strength to the earth."*

9. **Psalm 9:12**—*When He avenges blood, He remembers them; He does not forget the cry of the humble.*

10. **Numbers 35:9-34**—*Then the* LORD *spoke to Moses, saying,* [10] *"Speak to the children of Israel, and say to them: 'When you cross the Jordan into the land of Canaan,* [11] *then you shall appoint cities to be cities of refuge for you, that the manslayer who kills any person accidentally may flee there.* [12] *They shall be cities of refuge for you from the avenger, that the manslayer may not die until he stands before the congregation in judgment.* [13] *And of the cities which you give, you shall have six cities of refuge.* [14] *You shall appoint three cities on this side of the Jordan, and three cities you shall appoint in the land of Canaan, which will be cities of refuge.* [15] *These six cities shall be for refuge for the children of Israel, for the stranger, and for the sojourner among them, that anyone who kills a person accidentally may flee there.* [16] *But if he strikes him with an iron implement, so that he dies, he is a murderer; the murderer shall surely be put to death.* [17] *And if he strikes him with a stone in the hand, by which one could die, and he does die, he is a murderer; the murderer shall surely be put to death.* [18] *Or if he strikes him with a wooden hand weapon, by which one could die, and he does die, he is a murderer; the murderer shall surely be put to death.* [19] ***The avenger of blood himself shall put the murderer to death****; when he meets him, he shall put him to death.* [20] *If he pushes him out of hatred or, while lying in wait, hurls something at him so that he dies,* [21] *or in enmity he strikes*

him with his hand so that he dies, the one who struck him shall surely be put to death. He is a murderer. ***The avenger of blood shall put the murderer to death when he meets him.*** *[22] However, if he pushes him suddenly without enmity, or throws anything at him without lying in wait, [23] or uses a stone, by which a man could die, throwing it at him without seeing him, so that he dies, while he was not his enemy or seeking his harm, [24] then the congregation shall judge between the manslayer and the avenger of blood according to these judgments. [25] So the congregation shall deliver the manslayer from the hand of the avenger of blood, and the congregation shall return him to the city of refuge where he had fled, and he shall remain there until the death of the high priest who was anointed with the holy oil. [26] But if the manslayer at any time goes outside the limits of the city of refuge where he fled, [27]* ***and the avenger of blood finds him outside the limits of his city of refuge, and the avenger of blood kills the manslayer, he shall not be guilty of blood,*** *[28] because he should have remained in his city of refuge until the death of the high priest. But after the death of the high priest the manslayer may return to the land of his possession. [29] And these things shall be a statute of judgment to you throughout your generations in all your dwellings. [30] Whoever kills a person, the murderer shall be put to death on the testimony of witnesses; but one witness is not sufficient testimony against a person for the death penalty. [31] Moreover you shall take no ransom for the life of a murderer who is guilty of death, but he shall surely be put to death. [32] And you shall take no ransom for him who has fled to his city of refuge, that he may return to dwell in the land before the death of the priest. [33] So you shall not pollute the land where you are; for blood defiles the land, and no atonement can be made for the land, for the blood that is shed on it, except by the blood of him who shed it. [34] Therefore do not defile the land which you inhabit, in the midst of which I dwell; for I the* L*ORD* *dwell among the children of Israel.'"*

11. **Revelation 19:13-14**—*He was* ***clothed with a robe dipped in blood,*** *and His name is called The Word of God. [14] And the armies in heaven, clothed in fine linen, white and clean, followed Him on white horses.*

12. **Psalm 24:7-10 KJV**—*Lift up your heads, O ye gates; and be ye lift up, ye everlasting doors; and the King of glory shall come in. [8] Who is this King of glory? The* L*ORD* *strong and mighty, the Lord mighty in battle. [9] Lift up your heads, O ye gates; even lift them up, ye everlasting doors; and the King of glory shall come in. [10] Who is this King of glory? The* L*ORD* *of hosts, he is the King of glory. Selah.*

13. **John 20:11-18 KJV**—*But Mary stood without at the sepulchre weeping: and as she wept, she stooped down, and looked into the sepulchre, [12] and seeth two angels in white sitting, the one at the head, and the other at the feet, where the body of Jesus had lain. [13] And they say*

> *unto her, Woman, why weepest thou? She saith unto them, Because they have taken away my Lord, and I know not where they have laid him. [14] And when she had thus said, she turned herself back, and saw Jesus standing, and knew not that it was Jesus. [15] Jesus saith unto her, Woman, why weepest thou? whom seekest thou? She, supposing him to be the gardener, saith unto him, Sir, if thou have borne him hence, tell me where thou hast laid him, and I will take him away. [16] Jesus saith unto her, Mary. She turned herself, and saith unto him, Rabboni; which is to say, Master. [17]* ***Jesus saith unto her, Touch me not; for I am not yet ascended to my Father****: but go to my brethren, and say unto them, I ascend unto my Father, and your Father; and to my God, and your God. [18] Mary Magdalene came and told the disciples that she had seen the Lord, and that he had spoken these things unto her.*

Read Philippians 2:10-11 and Romans 14:11. When Jesus returns at the end of the Great Tribulation, people will recognize that Jesus is the Son of God and the only way to the Father. What do these verses say will happen among all people?

____

____

____

____

____

THE FIERCE WRATH OF THE LAMB

People have longed to see God, to know and experience Him. In Exodus 33:18, Moses asked to see God's glory. God didn't show Moses His face. Instead, He hid him in the cleft of the rock, and Moses saw the Lord's back. God desires to reveal Himself to His children. The scenario is different in Revelation 6:15-16: the fear everyone alive at that time will feel will be so intense that they will go into hiding. These people won't want any part of God. Why do you think this is their response, which differs from Moses' in Exodus 33:18 and Revelation 6:15-16?

____

____

____

____

____

EVERY EYE WILL SEE HIM

The idea that every eye will see Jesus when He comes back is quite extraordinary. How do you think this will take place? Supernaturally or virtually? Write down your thoughts.

____

____

____

____

____

____

PROPHETIC SCRIPTURES SHOWING THE WHOLE WORLD WILL BE IMPACTED BY JESUS' RETURN

Several scriptures in this section describe Jesus as the Son of Man. Why do you think He is given this title? If you would like, do a little research and write what you find about why He is called this.

____

____

____

____

____

THE BATTLE OF EDOM

FOCUS POINT

Isaiah 63:1-6 reveals that Jesus will take a detour and stop at Edom's capital. He does this to rescue those surrounded by the enemy. Jesus steps in and singlehandedly destroys everyone holding His people hostage and entrapping them. The Lord's ears are always attuned to His children. Psalm 34:17-18 says, "*The righteous cry out, and the Lord hears, and delivers them out of all their troubles.* [18] *The Lord is near to those who have a broken heart, and saves such as have a contrite spirit.*" This is a promise from God, and it continues even after the Great Tribulation. His love for His children is so great that He will rescue them from all their troubles.

Take a moment and reflect on this. Are you facing things that you need to be delivered from? If so, take this time to write them down and speak Psalm 34:17-18 over your situation.

____

____

____

____

____

____

____

____

____

____

____

AVENGER OF BLOOD

In the Bible, an avenger of blood is a person legally responsible for carrying out vengeance when a family member has been unlawfully killed or murdered. The avenger of blood is usually the nearest male relative of the murdered person. This family executioner seeks justice by killing the individual responsible for the death of his relative. The word translated "avenge," in Hebrew, is related to the word for "redeem," "reclaim," or "restore." As a representative of God and the family, the avenger of blood "redeemed" or "reclaimed" the blood of the relative by killing the original blood-shedder.[1] Isaiah 63:1-6 reveals that Jesus will be the avenger of blood for His people. He will be redeeming, reclaiming, and restoring those He is avenging.

ROBE DIPPED IN BLOOD

It will be quite the sight when Jesus arrives at the Battle of Armageddon with His robe dipped in blood. Not only will He be coming ready for war, but His appearance will reveal that He has already been in a tremendous fight. What do you think the enemy will be thinking when they see Jesus?

FAITH CAN INTERRUPT GOD

When Jesus died on the cross and was resurrected, He took the keys of death, hell, and the grave. When He comes at the end of the Tribulation, He will not only defeat the enemy but also have the final say for all eternity. What similarities are there between those rescued from Abraham's bosom and those being rescued at the Battle of Armageddon?

MARY INTERRUPTED JESUS' PARADE

Jesus paused His procession to heaven to meet with Mary. She was pulling on Him in the Spirit with such urgency. Jesus loves us so much that when we need Him, He is right there. Many would say He is unavailable or too busy. However, in this situation, Jesus took the time to show Mary how important she was. Throughout your life, write about a time when you were in a desperate situation and needed an encounter with Jesus.

THE END OF AN AGE

PERSONAL REFLECTIONS

Jesus is coming for His bride, the Church. We need to be ready. Those who don't have Jesus as their Lord and Savior will be left behind. Second Peter 3:9 says, "The Lord is not slack concerning His promise, as some count slackness, but is longsuffering toward us, not willing that any should perish but that all should come to repentance." God desires that no one perish but that all be saved.

The purpose of this book is to raise awareness of what lies ahead. Second Corinthians 6:2 says, *"For He says, 'In an acceptable time I have heard you, and in the day of salvation I have helped you.' Behold, now is the accepted time; behold, now is the day of salvation."* Today is the day of salvation. Why? Because you are not guaranteed tomorrow. If you have not accepted Jesus as your Savior, please take a moment to do so right now. Pray the following prayer:

Lord, I confess that I have sinned and need a Savior. I believe in my heart, without doubt, that You, Jesus, died for me to forgive all my sins—past, present, and future. I believe God raised You from the dead, and You are seated at His right hand. I call on the name of the Lord. Thank You that I am saved!

If you prayed this, please reach out to our office at info@zministries.com, and we will send you our teaching titled *Saved, Rescued for a Purpose*. Welcome to the family!

CHAPTER TWO

ANCIENT EARTH AND LUCIFER'S FLOOD

SCRIPTURES

1. **Ecclesiastes 1:9-11**—*That which has been is what will be, that which is done is what will be done, and there is nothing new under the sun.* [10] *Is there anything of which it may be said, "See, this is new"? It has already been in ancient times before us.* [11] *There is no remembrance of former things, nor will there be any remembrance of things that are to come by those who will come after.*

2. **Deuteronomy 29:29**—*The secret things belong to the* LORD *our God, but those things which are revealed belong to us and to our children forever, that we may do all the words of this law.*

3. **Proverbs 25:2**—*It is the glory of God to conceal a matter, but the glory of kings is to search out a matter.*

4. **First Corinthians 4:6**—*Now these things, brethren, I have figuratively transferred to myself and Apollos for your sakes, that you may learn in us not to think beyond what is written, that none of you may be puffed up on behalf of one against the other.*

5. **Psalm 90:4 NIV**—***A thousand years*** *in your sight are like a* ***day*** *that has just gone by, or like a watch in the night.*

6. **Second Peter 3:8 NIV**—*But do not forget this one thing, dear friends: With the Lord a* ***day*** *is like a* ***thousand years,*** *and a* ***thousand years*** *are like a* ***day****.*

7. **Genesis 1:1-2 NIV**—*In the beginning God created the heavens and the earth. [2] Now the earth was formless and empty, darkness was over the surface of the deep, and the Spirit of God was hovering over the waters.*

8. **Ezekiel 28:12-14 NIV**—*Son of man, take up a lament concerning the king of Tyre and say to him: "This is what the Sovereign Lord says: 'You were the seal of perfection, full of wisdom and perfect in beauty. [13] You were in Eden, the garden of God; every precious stone adorned you: carnelian, chrysolite and emerald, topaz, onyx and jasper, lapis lazuli, turquoise and beryl. Your settings and mountings were made of gold; on the day you were created they were prepared. [14]* ***You were anointed as a guardian cherub****, for so I ordained you. You were on the holy mount of God; you walked among the fiery stones.'"*

9. **Revelation 12:3-9**—*And another sign appeared in heaven: behold, a great, fiery red dragon having seven heads and ten horns, and seven diadems on his heads. [4] His tail drew a third of the stars of heaven and threw them to the earth. And the dragon stood before the woman who was ready to give birth, to devour her Child as soon as it was born. [5] She bore a male Child who was to rule all nations with a rod of iron. And her Child was caught up to God and His throne. [6] Then the woman fled into the wilderness, where she has a place prepared by God, that they should feed her there one thousand two hundred and sixty days. [7] And war broke out in heaven: Michael and his angels fought with the dragon; and the dragon and his angels fought, [8] but they did not prevail, nor was a place found for them in heaven any longer. [9] So the great dragon was cast out, that serpent of old, called the Devil and Satan, who deceives the whole world; he was cast to the earth, and his angels were cast out with him.*

10. **Ezekiel 28:15-18 NIV**—*You were* ***blameless*** *in your ways from the day you were created till* ***wickedness*** *was found in you. [16] Through your widespread trade you were filled with* ***violence*** *and you sinned. So I drove you in disgrace from the mount of God, and I expelled you, guardian cherub, from among the fiery stones. [17] Your heart became* ***proud*** *on account of your beauty, and you* ***corrupted*** *your wisdom because of your splendor. So I threw you to the earth; I made a spectacle of you before kings. [18] By your* ***many sins*** *and* ***dishonest trade*** *you have desecrated your sanctuaries. So I made a fire come out from you, and it consumed you, and I reduced you to ashes on the ground in the sight of all who were watching.*

11. **Isaiah 14:12-15**—*How you are fallen from heaven, O Lucifer, son of the morning! How you are cut down to the ground, you who weakened the nations! [13] For you have said in your heart: "I will ascend into heaven, I will exalt my throne above the stars of God; I will*

also sit on the mount of the congregation on the farthest sides of the north; [14] *I will ascend above the heights of the clouds, I will be like the Most High."* [15] *Yet you shall be brought down to Sheol, to the lowest depths of the Pit.*

12. **Second Peter 2:4**—*For if God did not spare the angels who sinned, but cast them down to hell and delivered them into chains of darkness, to be reserved for judgment.*

13. **Luke 10:18**—*And He said to them, "I saw Satan fall like lightning from heaven."*

14. **Isaiah 14:12**—*How you are fallen from heaven, O Lucifer, son of the morning! How you are cut down to the ground, you who weakened the nations!*

15. **Isaiah 14:16-20**—*Those who see you will gaze at you, and consider you, saying: "Is this the man who made the earth tremble, who shook kingdoms,* [17] *who made the world as a wilderness and destroyed its cities, who did not open the house of his prisoners?"* [18] *All the kings of the nations, all of them, sleep in glory, everyone in his own house;* [19] ***But you are cast out of your grave like an abominable branch, like the garment of those who are slain, thrust through with a sword, who go down to the stones of the pit, like a corpse trodden underfoot.*** [20] *You will not be joined with them in burial, because you have destroyed your land and slain your people. The brood of evildoers shall never be named.*

16. **Ezekiel 28:19 NIV**—*All the nations who knew you are appalled at you; you have come to a horrible end and will be no more.*

17. **Revelation 20:10**—*The devil, who deceived them, was cast into the lake of fire and brimstone where the beast and the false prophet are. And they will be tormented day and night forever and ever.*

18. **Genesis 1:2 NIV**—*Now the earth* ***was*** *formless and empty, darkness was over the surface of the deep, and the Spirit of God was hovering over the waters.*

19. **Exodus 9:24**—*So there was hail, and fire mingled with the hail, so very heavy that there was none like it in all the land of Egypt since it became a nation.*

20. **Genesis 19:26**—*But his wife looked back behind him, and she became a pillar of salt.*

21. **Genesis 1:28 KJV**—*And God blessed them, and God said unto them, Be fruitful, and multiply, and* ***replenish*** *the earth, and subdue it: and have dominion over the fish of the sea, and over the fowl of the air, and over every living thing that moveth upon the earth.*

22. **Matthew 24:37-39**—*But as the days of Noah* ***were,*** *so also will the coming of the Son of Man be.* [38] *For as in the days before the flood, they were eating and drinking, marrying and giving in marriage, until the day that Noah entered the ark,* [39] *and did not know until the flood came and took them all away, so also will the coming of the Son of Man be.*

23. **Second Peter 3:5-7**—*For this they willfully forget: that by the word of God the heavens were of old, and the earth standing out of water and in the water,* [6] *by which the world that then existed perished, being flooded with water.* [7] *But the heavens and the earth which are now preserved by the same word, are reserved for fire until the day of judgment and perdition of ungodly men.*

24. **Isaiah 45:18**—*For thus says the* LORD, *who created the heavens, who is God, who formed the earth and made it, who has established it, who did not create it in vain, who formed it to be inhabited: "I am the* LORD, *and there is no other."*

25. **Jeremiah 4:23-26**—*I beheld the earth, and indeed it was without form, and void; and the heavens, they had no light.* [24] *I beheld the mountains, and indeed they trembled, and all the hills moved back and forth.* [25] *I beheld, and indeed there was no man, and all the birds of the heavens had fled.* [26] *I beheld, and indeed the fruitful land was a wilderness, and all its cities were broken down at the presence of the* LORD, *by His fierce anger.*

26. **Psalm 104:5-9**—*You who laid the foundations of the earth, so that it should not be moved forever,* [6] *You covered it with the deep as with a garment; the waters stood above the mountains.* [7] *At Your rebuke they fled; at the voice of Your thunder they hastened away.* [8] *They went up over the mountains; they went down into the valleys, to the place which You founded for them.* [9] *You have set a boundary that they may not pass over, that they may not return to cover the earth.*

27. **Genesis 1:3-31**—*Then God said, "Let there be light"; and there was light.* [4] *And God saw the light, that it was good; and God divided the light from the darkness.* [5] *God called the light Day, and the darkness He called Night. So the evening and the morning were the first day.* [6] *Then God said, "Let there be a firmament in the midst of the waters, and let it divide the waters from the waters."* [7] *Thus God made the firmament, and divided the waters which were under the firmament from the waters which were above the firmament; and it was so.* [8] *And God called the firmament heaven. So the evening and the morning were the second day.* [9] *Then God said, "Let the waters under the heavens be gathered together into one place, and let the dry land appear"; and it was so.* [10] *And God called the dry land earth, and the gathering*

together of the waters He called Seas. And God saw that it was good. [11] Then God said, "Let the earth bring forth grass, the herb that yields seed, and the fruit tree that yields fruit according to its kind, whose seed is in itself, on the earth"; and it was so. [12] And the earth brought forth grass, the herb that yields seed according to its kind, and the tree that yields fruit, whose seed is in itself according to its kind. And God saw that it was good. [13] So the evening and the morning were the third day. [14] Then God said, "Let there be lights in the firmament of the heavens to divide the day from the night; and let them be for signs and seasons, and for days and years; [15] and let them be for lights in the firmament of the heavens to give light on the earth"; and it was so. [16] Then God made two great lights: the greater light to rule the day, and the lesser light to rule the night. He made the stars also. [17] God set them in the firmament of the heavens to give light on the earth, [18] and to rule over the day and over the night, and to divide the light from the darkness. And God saw that it was good. [19] So the evening and the morning were the fourth day. [20] Then God said, "Let the waters abound with an abundance of living creatures, and let birds fly above the earth across the face of the firmament of the heavens." [21] So God created great sea creatures and every living thing that moves, with which the waters abounded, according to their kind, and every winged bird according to its kind. And God saw that it was good. [22] And God blessed them, saying, "Be fruitful and multiply, and fill the waters in the seas, and let birds multiply on the earth." [23] So the evening and the morning were the fifth day. [24] Then God said, "Let the earth bring forth the living creature according to its kind: cattle and creeping thing and beast of the earth, each according to its kind"; and it was so. [25] And God made the beast of the earth according to its kind, cattle according to its kind, and everything that creeps on the earth according to its kind. And God saw that it was good. [26] Then God said, "Let Us make man in Our image, according to Our likeness; let them have dominion over the fish of the sea, over the birds of the air, and over the cattle, over all the earth and over every creeping thing that creeps on the earth." [27] So God created man in His own image; in the image of God He created him; male and female He created them. [28] Then God blessed them, and God said to them, "Be fruitful and multiply; fill the earth and subdue it; have dominion over the fish of the sea, over the birds of the air, and over every living thing that moves on the earth." [29] And God said, "See, I have given you every herb that yields seed which is on the face of all the earth, and every tree whose fruit yields seed; to you it shall be for food. [30] Also, to every beast of the earth, to every bird of the air, and to everything that creeps on the earth, in which there is life, I have given every green herb for food"; and it was so. [31] Then God saw everything that He had made, and indeed it was very good. So the evening and the morning were the sixth day.

28. **Genesis 2:1-25**—*Thus the heavens and the earth, and all the host of them, were finished. [2] And on the seventh day God ended His work which He had done, and He rested on*

the seventh day from all His work which He had done. 3 Then God blessed the seventh day and sanctified it, because in it He rested from all His work which God had created and made. 4 This is the history of the heavens and the earth when they were created, in the day that the LORD God made the earth and the heavens, 5 before any plant of the field was in the earth and before any herb of the field had grown. For the LORD God had not caused it to rain on the earth, and there was no man to till the ground; 6 but a mist went up from the earth and watered the whole face of the ground. 7 And the LORD God formed man of the dust of the ground, and breathed into his nostrils the breath of life; and man became a living being. 8 The LORD God planted a garden eastward in Eden, and there He put the man whom He had formed. 9 And out of the ground the LORD God made every tree grow that is pleasant to the sight and good for food. The tree of life was also in the midst of the garden, and the tree of the knowledge of good and evil. 10 Now a river went out of Eden to water the garden, and from there it parted and became four riverheads. 11 The name of the first is Pishon; it is the one which skirts the whole land of Havilah, where there is gold. 12 And the gold of that land is good. Bdellium and the onyx stone are there. 13 The name of the second river is Gihon; it is the one which goes around the whole land of Cush. 14 The name of the third river is Hiddekel; it is the one which goes toward the east of Assyria. The fourth river is the Euphrates. 15 Then the LORD God took the man and put him in the garden of Eden to tend and keep it. 16 And the LORD God commanded the man, saying, "Of every tree of the garden you may freely eat; 17 but of the tree of the knowledge of good and evil you shall not eat, for in the day that you eat of it you shall surely die." 18 And the LORD God said, "It is not good that man should be alone; I will make him a helper comparable to him." 19 Out of the ground the LORD God formed every beast of the field and every bird of the air, and brought them to Adam to see what he would call them. And whatever Adam called each living creature, that was its name. 20 So Adam gave names to all cattle, to the birds of the air, and to every beast of the field. But for Adam there was not found a helper comparable to him. 21 And the LORD God caused a deep sleep to fall on Adam, and he slept; and He took one of his ribs, and closed up the flesh in its place. 22 Then the rib which the LORD God had taken from man He made into a woman, and He brought her to the man. 23 And Adam said: "This is now bone of my bones and flesh of my flesh; she shall be called Woman, because she was taken out of Man." 24 Therefore a man shall leave his father and mother and be joined to his wife, and they shall become one flesh. 25 And they were both naked, the man and his wife, and were not ashamed.

THERE IS NOTHING NEW UNDER THE SUN!

Ecclesiastes 1:9-11 reveals that there is nothing new under the sun. This means that everything we see today reflects, in some way, what has been done in the past. This understanding applies to a person's daily life. No matter what you're experiencing, chances are someone else has gone through a similar situation. There is a scripture for every challenge you face. Use God's Word and speak it aloud over your circumstances. You will always come out victorious!

NO REMEMBRANCE OF THE FORMER THINGS

It is interesting to think that former things will not be remembered. Why do you think God created this process of forgetting previous things? Could this be a helpful tool for humanity? What are your thoughts?

____

____

____

____

____

____

THE SECRET THINGS BELONG TO THE LORD. CONCEALED THINGS ARE MEANT TO BE SEARCHED OUT

FOCUS POINT

But seek first the kingdom of God and His righteousness, and all these things shall be added to you.

—Matthew 6:33

The Lord reveals His secrets to His children. Matthew 6:33 says we are to seek the kingdom of God and His righteousness first, and then all things will be added to us. These "things" could be the secret things that belong to the Lord. He desires to be sought after and pursued. As Proverbs 25:2 shows, the glory of God conceals a matter, but the glory of kings is to search it out. What does that mean? God's glory reveals itself through His concealed wisdom and methods, whereas human honor—particularly for leaders—stems from examining, discovering facts, and pursuing truth to make wise choices. This contrast highlights the beautiful difference between divine transcendence and our shared responsibility to lead with fairness. It fosters faith, as God hides certain things to motivate His people to seek Him more deeply and grow spiritually, making the process of discovery commendable. God desires fellowship. Take this time to seek Him and spend time with Him.

OLD EARTH CREATIONISM

According to Psalm 90:4 and 2 Peter 3:8, the word "day" is described as a thousand years. What are your thoughts on the creation story taking longer than six days if this theory is used?

LUCIFER'S ROLE

Lucifer was anointed and ordained. This means that God chose, set apart, and appointed him for a special purpose, to be the guardian cherub who governed the earth alongside God. This position was the highest one could be appointed to. He walked with God and among fiery stones. What do you think these stones are?

LUCIFER WAS COVERED IN PRECIOUS STONES

Imagine Lucifer's beauty, adorned with every precious stone and gold. Exodus describes him as perfect in beauty. What details about his garment catch your attention now that you might not have noticed before?

LUCIFER, THE WORSHIP LEADER IN HEAVEN

Knowing that Lucifer may have been the worship leader in heaven can reveal his influence on music culture today. How do you think he is involved in the music we see in the secular world and in Christian music?

THE REBELLION AND FALL

Lucifer went from blameless to outright wicked. To think that the highest-ranking cherub, possibly the worship leader, decided to go rogue and leave everything. How do you think this happens in someone's heart? Have you ever witnessed this in someone close to you? If so, what were the identifiable changes in that person?

TRUE EVIL AND VIOLENCE

Violence and pride are two forces that can corrupt anyone. One might ask, "Was Lucifer violent toward those around him? Did he harm the other angels?" This is an interesting question. His self-love bred such pride that his wisdom was corrupted. Why do you think violence and pride can corrupt someone's wisdom?

LUCIFER HAD A LOVE OF MONEY AND WAS FILLED WITH GREED

Lucifer treated his sanctuaries with such disgrace and disrespect. He turned something holy into something profane. This defilement led to dishonest trade. Have you seen someone's sin affect how they operate at work? If so, why do you think this is a normal process for those living in sin?

GREED WAS AN ISSUE THAT MADE LUCIFER WANT TO BE LIKE GOD HIMSELF!

Lucifer truly believed he had a chance to be like God. How does someone reach a point of being so deceived in their heart and mind that they believe something impossible can be attained and even become true?

____

____

____

____

____

____

THE HORRIFIC FATE OF SATAN

We know what Satan's fate is. As stated, Satan influenced one-third of the angels in heaven to join him. How could someone who was violent, corrupt, and full of pride persuade angels to leave their God-assigned posts and join him? Satan has been deceiving the masses from the beginning. How do you think this influence still operates today?

____

____

____

____

____

____

A FIRE CAME FROM WITHIN LUCIFER, WHICH LIKELY BURNED AWAY HIS GLORY

To understand what it means that Satan's glory was burned away, one needs to know what glory is. Lucifer's glory was that he was God's most magnificent creation up to that point. He was the "seal of perfection," full of wisdom and beauty, the highest-ranking angel, and described as a radiant "morning star." All of these described who he was, and in that moment, they were all burned away. Consumed by the intense fire, he left a pitiful sight for all to see.

COMMENTS OF THOSE WHO SEE HIM IN HIS DEMOTED STATE

The devil's appearance will surprise everyone. What do you think people's response will be when they see him for who he truly is at the end of the age? How can this understanding help believers who are currently afraid of him?

FINAL DESTINATION—THE LAKE OF FIRE

Newton's Third Law of Motion states that for every action, there is an equal and opposite reaction.[1] With this understanding, everything Lucifer did (action) produced a consequence (reaction). Hell will be such a reaction. The lake of fire will also be the punishment (reaction) for all he will do up to that point. His destination will be eternal separation from God, and his earthly influence will be stopped forever. Thank God for that!

EARTH AFTER ANCIENT JUDGMENT AND DESTRUCTION

Looking at the definition of "was" and its tie to the meaning "become," what are your thoughts on these words and the possibility that there was a previous earth that became *formless and empty*?

PRE-ADAMIC ERA

After reading the previous sections in the main book, what are your thoughts on a pre-Adamic civilization existing before Genesis 1:2?

REPLENISH THE EARTH OR BUILD IT UP AGAIN

In Genesis 1:28, the word "replenish" supports the argument that there was a pre-Adam and Eve society. What do you think about this idea? Write your thoughts and state your stance.

FINIS DAKE'S INSIGHT ON LUCIFER'S FLOOD

After reading Finis Dake's thoughts on the Luciferian Flood and Noah's Flood, what are your thoughts concerning the two?

LUCIFER'S FLOOD DESTROYED EARTH, LEAVING IT WITHOUT FORM AND VOID. NOTHING WAS LEFT—ONLY DARKNESS!

PERSONAL REFLECTIONS

Lucifer's rebellion, sin, and vile acts led to the destruction of what some call the Old Earth. He is a prime example of how these things, when they appear in someone's life, bring consequences. The opposite is true for those living a righteous life. First Peter 1:13-16 says, "Therefore gird up the loins of your mind, be sober, and rest your hope fully upon the grace that is to be brought to you at the revelation of Jesus Christ; 14 as obedient children, not conforming yourselves to the former lusts, as in your ignorance; 15 but as He who called you is holy, you also be holy in all your conduct, 16 because it is written, 'Be holy, for I am holy.'" Take this time of reflection and ask the Lord to help you in your walk of imitating Him, to be holy as He is. Write down your thoughts and prayers.

CHAPTER THREE

YOUNG EARTH CREATIONIST THEORY

SCRIPTURES

1. **Genesis 1:1**—*In the beginning God created the heavens and the earth.*

2. **Genesis 1:2-31 NIV**—*Now the earth was formless and empty, darkness was over the
surface of the deep, and the Spirit of God was hovering over the waters. 3 And God said, "Let
there be light," and there was light. 4 God saw that the light was good, and he separated the
light from the darkness. 5 God called the light "**day**," and the darkness he called "night." And
there was evening, and there was morning—the first **day**. 6 And God said, "Let there be a
vault between the waters to separate water from water." 7 So God made the vault and separated
the water under the vault from the water above it. And it was so. 8 God called the vault "sky."
And there was evening, and there was morning—the second **day**. 9 And God said, "Let the
water under the sky be gathered to one place, and let dry ground appear." And it was so. 10 God
called the dry ground "land," and the gathered waters he called "seas." And God saw that it
was good. 11 Then God said, "Let the land produce vegetation: seed-bearing plants and trees on
the land that bear fruit with seed in it, according to their various kinds." And it was so. 12 The
land produced vegetation: plants bearing seed according to their kinds and trees bearing fruit
with seed in it according to their kinds. And God saw that it was good. 13 And there was eve-
ning, and there was morning—the third **day**. 14 And God said, "Let there be lights in the vault
of the sky to separate the day from the night, and let them serve as signs to mark sacred times,
and days and years, 15 and let them be lights in the vault of the sky to give light on the earth."
And it was so. 16 God made two great lights—the greater light to govern the day and the lesser
light to govern the night. He also made the stars. 17 God set them in the vault of the sky to*

give light on the earth, [18] *to govern the day and the night, and to separate light from darkness. And God saw that it was good.* [19] *And there was evening, and there was morning—the fourth* ***day****.* [20] *And God said, "Let the water teem with living creatures, and let birds fly above the earth across the vault of the sky."* [21] *So God created the great creatures of the sea and every living thing with which the water teems and that moves about in it, according to their kinds, and every winged bird according to its kind. And God saw that it was good.* [22] *God blessed them and said, "Be fruitful and increase in number and fill the water in the seas, and let the birds increase on the earth."* [23] *And there was evening, and there was morning—the fifth* ***day****.* [24] *And God said, "Let the land produce living creatures according to their kinds: the livestock, the creatures that move along the ground, and the wild animals, each according to its kind." And it was so.* [25] *God made the wild animals according to their kinds, the livestock according to their kinds, and all the creatures that move along the ground according to their kinds. And God saw that it was good.* [26] *Then God said, "Let us make mankind in our image, in our likeness, so that they may rule over the fish in the sea and the birds in the sky, over the livestock and all the wild animals, and over all the creatures that move along the ground."* [27] *So God created mankind in his own image, in the image of God he created them; male and female he created them.* [28] *God blessed them and said to them, "Be fruitful and increase in number; fill the earth and subdue it. Rule over the fish in the sea and the birds in the sky and over every living creature that moves on the ground."* [29] *Then God said, "I give you every seed-bearing plant on the face of the whole earth and every tree that has fruit with seed in it. They will be yours for food.* [30] *And to all the beasts of the earth and all the birds in the sky and all the creatures that move along the ground—everything that has the breath of life in it—I give every green plant for food." And it was so.* [31] *God saw all that he had made, and it was very good. And there was evening, and there was morning—the sixth* ***day****.*

3. **Genesis 1:28 KJV**—*And God blessed them, and God said unto them, Be fruitful, and multiply, and* ***replenish*** *the earth, and subdue it: and have dominion over the fish of the sea, and over the fowl of the air, and over every living thing that moveth upon the earth.*

4. **Genesis 1:28**—*Then God blessed them, and God said to them, "Be fruitful and multiply;* ***fill*** *the earth and subdue it; have dominion over the fish of the sea, over the birds of the air, and over every living thing that moves on the earth."*

5. **Genesis 5–11**—*Due to the length of the text, please read from your Bible.*

6. **Matthew 1:1-25**—*The book of the genealogy of Jesus Christ, the Son of David, the Son of Abraham:* [2] *Abraham begot Isaac, Isaac begot Jacob, and Jacob begot Judah and his brothers.*

[3]*Judah begot Perez and Zerah by Tamar, Perez begot Hezron, and Hezron begot Ram.* [4]
Ram begot Amminadab, Amminadab begot Nahshon, and Nahshon begot Salmon. [5] *Salmon*
begot Boaz by Rahab, Boaz begot Obed by Ruth, Obed begot Jesse, [6] *and Jesse begot David*
the king. David the king begot Solomon by her **who had been the wife** *of Uriah.* [7] *Solomon*
begot Rehoboam, Rehoboam begot Abijah, and Abijah begot Asa. [8] *Asa begot Jehoshaphat,*
Jehoshaphat begot Joram, and Joram begot Uzziah. [9] *Uzziah begot Jotham, Jotham begot*
Ahaz, and Ahaz begot Hezekiah. [10] *Hezekiah begot Manasseh, Manasseh begot Amon, and*
Amon begot Josiah. [11] *Josiah begot Jeconiah and his brothers about the time they were carried*
away to Babylon. [12] *And after they were brought to Babylon, Jeconiah begot Shealtiel, and*
Shealtiel begot Zerubbabel. [13] *Zerubbabel begot Abiud, Abiud begot Eliakim, and Eliakim*
begot Azor. [14] *Azor begot Zadok, Zadok begot Achim, and Achim begot Eliud.* [15] *Eliud begot*
Eleazar, Eleazar begot Matthan, and Matthan begot Jacob. [16] *And Jacob begot Joseph the*
husband of Mary, of whom was born Jesus who is called Christ. [17] *So all the generations from*
Abraham to David **are** *fourteen generations, from David until the captivity in Babylon* **are**
fourteen generations, and from the captivity in Babylon until the Christ **are** *fourteen genera-*
tions. [18] *Now the birth of Jesus Christ was as follows: After His mother Mary was betrothed to*
Joseph, before they came together, she was found with child of the Holy Spirit. [19] *Then Joseph*
her husband, being a just **man,** *and not wanting to make her a public example, was minded*
to put her away secretly. [20] *But while he thought about these things, behold, an angel of the*
Lord appeared to him in a dream, saying, "Joseph, son of David, do not be afraid to take to
you Mary your wife, for that which is conceived in her is of the Holy Spirit. [21] *And she will*
bring forth a Son, and you shall call His name JESUS, for He will save His people from their
sins." [22] *So all this was done that it might be fulfilled which was spoken by the Lord through*
the prophet, saying: [23] *"Behold, the virgin shall be with child, and bear a Son, and they shall*
call His name Immanuel," which is translated, "God with us." [24] *Then Joseph, being aroused*
from sleep, did as the angel of the Lord commanded him and took to him his wife, [25] *and did*
not know her till she had brought forth her firstborn Son. And he called His name JESUS.

7. **Luke 3:1-38**—*Now in the fifteenth year of the reign of Tiberius Caesar, Pontius Pilate*
being governor of Judea, Herod being tetrarch of Galilee, his brother Philip tetrarch of Iturea
and the region of Trachonitis, and Lysanias tetrarch of Abilene, [2] *while Annas and Caiaphas*
were high priests, the word of God came to John the son of Zacharias in the wilderness. [3]
And he went into all the region around the Jordan, preaching a baptism of repentance for the
remission of sins, [4] *as it is written in the book of the words of Isaiah the prophet, saying: "The*
voice of one crying in the wilderness: 'Prepare the way of the LORD; make His paths straight.
[5] *Every valley shall be filled and every mountain and hill brought low; the crooked places shall*

be made straight and the rough ways smooth; 6 and all flesh shall see the salvation of God.'" 7 Then he said to the multitudes that came out to be baptized by him, "Brood of vipers! Who warned you to flee from the wrath to come? 8 Therefore bear fruits worthy of repentance, and do not begin to say to yourselves, 'We have Abraham as **our** *father.' For I say to you that God is able to raise up children to Abraham from these stones. 9 And even now the ax is laid to the root of the trees. Therefore every tree which does not bear good fruit is cut down and thrown into the fire." 10 So the people asked him, saying, "What shall we do then?" 11 He answered and said to them, "He who has two tunics, let him give to him who has none; and he who has food, let him do likewise." 12 Then tax collectors also came to be baptized, and said to him, "Teacher, what shall we do?" 13 And he said to them, "Collect no more than what is appointed for you." 14 Likewise the soldiers asked him, saying, "And what shall we do?" So he said to them, "Do not intimidate anyone or accuse falsely, and be content with your wages." 15 Now as the people were in expectation, and all reasoned in their hearts about John, whether he was the Christ* **or** *not, 16 John answered, saying to all, "I indeed baptize you with water; but One mightier than I is coming, whose sandal strap I am not worthy to loose. He will baptize you with the Holy Spirit and fire. 17 His winnowing fan* **is** *in His hand, and He will thoroughly clean out His threshing floor, and gather the wheat into His barn; but the chaff He will burn with unquenchable fire." 18 And with many other exhortations he preached to the people. 19 But Herod the tetrarch, being rebuked by him concerning Herodias, his brother Philip's wife, and for all the evils which Herod had done, 20 also added this, above all, that he shut John up in prison. 21 When all the people were baptized, it came to pass that Jesus also was baptized; and while He prayed, the heaven was opened. 22 And the Holy Spirit descended in bodily form like a dove upon Him, and a voice came from heaven which said, "You are My beloved Son; in You I am well pleased." 23 Now Jesus Himself began* **His ministry at** *about thirty years of age, being (as was supposed)* **the** *son of Joseph,* **the son** *of Heli, 24* **the son** *of Matthat,* **the son** *of Levi,* **the son** *of Melchi,* **the son** *of Janna,* **the son** *of Joseph, 25* **the son** *of Mattathiah,* **the son** *of Amos,* **the son** *of Nahum,* **the son** *of Esli,* **the son** *of Naggai, 26* **the son** *of Maath,* **the son** *of Mattathiah,* **the son** *of Semei,* **the son** *of Joseph,* **the son** *of Judah, 27* **the son** *of Joannas,* **the son** *of Rhesa,* **the son** *of Zerubbabel,* **the son** *of Shealtiel,* **the son** *of Neri, 28* **the son** *of Melchi,* **the son** *of Addi,* **the son** *of Cosam,* **the son** *of Elmodam,* **the son** *of Er, 29* **the son** *of Jose,* **the son** *of Eliezer,* **the son** *of Jorim,* **the son** *of Matthat,* **the son** *of Levi, 30* **the son** *of Simeon,* **the son** *of Judah,* **the son** *of Joseph,* **the son** *of Jonan,* **the son** *of Eliakim, 31* **the son** *of Melea,* **the son** *of Menan,* **the son** *of Mattathah,* **the son** *of Nathan,* **the son** *of David, 32* **the son** *of Jesse,* **the son** *of Obed,* **the son** *of Boaz,* **the son** *of Salmon,* **the son** *of Nahshon, 33* **the son** *of Amminadab,* **the son** *of Ram,* **the son** *of Hezron,* **the son** *of Perez,* **the son** *of Judah, 34* **the son** *of Jacob,* **the son** *of Isaac,* **the son** *of Abraham,* **the son** *of Terah,* ***the son*** *of Nahor,* [35] ***the son*** *of Serug,* ***the son*** *of Reu,* ***the son*** *of Peleg,* ***the son*** *of Eber,* ***the son*** *of Shelah,* [36] ***the son*** *of Cainan,* ***the son*** *of Arphaxad,* ***the son*** *of Shem,* ***the son*** *of Noah,* ***the son*** *of Lamech,* [37] ***the son*** *of Methuselah,* ***the son*** *of Enoch,* ***the son*** *of Jared,* ***the son*** *of Mahalalel,* ***the son*** *of Cainan,* [38] ***the son*** *of Enosh,* ***the son*** *of Seth,* ***the son*** *of Adam,* ***the son*** *of God.*

8. **Genesis 1:31**—*Then God saw everything that He had made, and indeed it was very good. So the evening and the morning were the sixth day.*

9. **Genesis 3:1-5**—*Now* ***the serpent was more cunning*** *than any beast of the field which the* LORD *God had made. And he said to the woman, "Has God indeed said, 'You shall not eat of every tree of the garden'?"* [2] *And the woman said to the serpent, "We may eat the fruit of the trees of the garden;* [3] *but of the fruit of the tree which is in the midst of the garden, God has said, 'You shall not eat it, nor shall you touch it, lest you die.'"* [4] *Then the serpent said to the woman, "You will not surely die.* [5] *For God knows that in the day you eat of it your eyes will be opened, and you will be like God, knowing good and evil."*

10. **Numbers 22:22-38**—*Due to the length of the text, please read from your Bible.*

11. **Genesis 3:21**—*Also for Adam and his wife the* LORD *God made tunics of skin, and clothed them.*

12. **Romans 5:12**—*Therefore, just as through one man sin entered the world, and death through sin, and thus death spread to all men, because all sinned.*

13. **Genesis 6:1-2**— *Now it came to pass, when men began to multiply on the face of the earth, and daughters were born to them,* [2] *that the sons of God saw the daughters of men, that they were beautiful; and they took wives for themselves of all whom they chose.*

14. **Genesis 6:5-7**—*Then the Lord saw that the wickedness of man was great in the earth, and that every intent of the thoughts of his heart was only evil continually.* [6] *And the* LORD *was sorry that He had made man on the earth, and He was grieved in His heart.* [7] *So the* LORD *said, "I will destroy man whom I have created from the face of the earth, both man and beast, creeping thing and birds of the air, for I am sorry that I have made them."*

15. **First Samuel 16:7**—*But the* LORD *said to Samuel, "Do not look at his appearance or at his physical stature, because I have refused him. For the* LORD *does not see as man sees; for man looks at the outward appearance, but the* LORD *looks at the heart."*

16. **Genesis 6:11-13**—*The earth also was corrupt before God, and the earth was filled with violence.* [12] *So God looked upon the earth, and indeed it was corrupt; for all flesh had corrupted their way on the earth.* [13] *And God said to Noah, "The end of all flesh has come before Me, for the earth is filled with violence through them; and behold, I will destroy them with the earth."*

17. **Genesis 6:4**—*There were* ***giants on the earth in those days, and also afterward****, when the sons of God came in to the daughters of men and they bore children to them. Those were the mighty men who were of old, men of renown.*

18. **Numbers 13:32-33**—*And they gave the children of Israel a bad report of the land which they had spied out, saying, "The land through which we have gone as spies is a land that devours its inhabitants, and all the people whom we saw in it are* ***men of great stature****.* [33] *There we saw* ***the giants*** *(the descendants of Anak came from the giants); and we were like grasshoppers in our own sight, and so we were in their sight."*

19. **John 10:10**—*The thief does not come except to steal, and to kill, and to destroy. I have come that they may have life, and that they may have it more abundantly.*

20. **Revelation 13:8**—*All who dwell on the earth will worship him, whose names have not been written in the Book of Life of the Lamb slain from the foundation of the world.*

A LITERAL 24-HOUR DAY

Genesis 1 describes the creation that took place over six days. Young Earth creationists believe this refers to literal 24-hour days. This differs from the thousands of years God would have taken to create, according to Old Earth creationists. What are your thoughts on this matter? Do you lean toward a literal day or a thousand-year creation narrative? List the reasons for your stance.

REPLENISH THE EARTH

FOCUS POINT

Genesis 1:28 says, "*Be fruitful and multiply.*" In this verse, God addresses population growth and the command to fill the earth and subdue it. Matthew 28:19-20 says, "'*Go therefore and make disciples of all the nations, baptizing them in the name of the Father and of the Son and of the Holy Spirit,* [20] *teaching them to observe all things that I have commanded you; and lo, I am with you always, even to the end of the age.*' *Amen.*" This is a form of multiplication. When we go into the world and make disciples, we take territory back from the enemy and spread the Word. This remains an ongoing mandate: to "raise a million to reach a billion." God has called us to reach the lost and disciple them, and those disciples will carry on the mission. Take a moment to ask the Holy Spirit whom you should reach out to and encourage today. Be sure to follow through and pray for them.

LUCIFER'S FALL

In the Young Earth theory, the timeline for Lucifer's iniquity to be born would have ranged from a few hours to 30 years. Do you find this timeline accurate? If so, write your thoughts as to why you come to that conclusion.

____

____

____

____

____

____

LUCIFER AS THE SERPENT

Lucifer tricked Eve into believing his voice over the Voice of God. Adam and Eve knew what God had said, yet they still chose to heed the word of the serpent. What do you think causes someone to set aside the truth for a lie?

____

____

DID THE ANIMALS SPEAK?

The book of Jubilees states that the mouths of animals were closed after Adam and Eve were removed from the Garden of Eden. What do you think the situation will be like in heaven for animals? Will they regain their ability to speak? If so, what are your thoughts on the matter?

FALLEN ANGELS AND THE CORRUPTION

Genesis 6 and 1 Enoch 6 share the same story about the angels, known as watchers, who saw the daughters of men and were struck by their beauty. This stirred great lust, which led them to leave their God-assigned posts. They chose sin and lust, similar to Satan, over everything God had given them. In 1 Enoch 6:3, the leader, Semjaza, told the others he was afraid they would not agree to do the deed and that he would be alone. This mirrors Satan's example, who convinced one-third of the angels to follow him. Semjaza and Lucifer were both persuasive, and others followed, giving up their rights to an eternity with God the Father, Jesus, and the Holy Spirit. When someone is so set on taking others to destruction, let this be a red flag to run the other way!

WATCHERS AND NEPHILIM

Once these angels married earthly women, a plan to corrupt the original seed was set in motion. Imagine a world where Nephilim walked, hundreds, if not thousands, of feet tall! These giants were so evil that they sinned against humankind and animals. The horror of what walked the earth at that time must have been so intense that humans tried to feed these giants whatever they could, only to protect themselves from being eaten by the giants. With this understanding, one can only agree that the flood was necessary!

DEFILEMENT BY WITCHCRAFT

Satan and these rebellious angels do not have the ability to create something from nothing; the only thing they are capable of is perverting what God has already created. With this in mind, what other things did God create for good, and how did the devil corrupt their use?

____

____

____

____

____

____

____

DESTRUCTION BY THE FLOOD OF NOAH

After reading the book of Jubilees 5:1-32, what stood out to you that you had not known before?

____

____

____

____

____

____

____

NOAH PLEASED GOD BY HAVING PURE BLOOD AND UNTAINTED DNA

Noah and his family's DNA were untainted. They were the only ones among all humanity at that time who stood their ground and kept their bloodline pure. Imagine the intensity of maintaining that stance. The pressure his family might have felt to take part in the evil going on was likely insurmountable. How do you think his family maintained their position and did not succumb to the cultural norms of their time?

CONCLUSION

PERSONAL REFLECTIONS

Revelation 13:8 reveals that Jesus was slain from the very beginning. He has been on a rescue mission since the fall of man. God has gone to great lengths to make a way for humanity to attain salvation and inherit eternal life with Him. When looking at the time after the watchmen left their posts and evil took hold to corrupt humankind, it's easy to see why God had to send the Flood. One can safely say, "Thank God for the Flood!" The plan of salvation for all mankind shows how much God loves people. Unfortunately, many will deny Him and choose the enemy's plan. Satan has been a liar from the beginning and will continue until he is thrown into the lake of fire. Till then, we need to be aware of his schemes and make sure we have ears to hear what the Spirit is saying. Take this time to learn to recognize God's Voice. If you are familiar with how He speaks, take this time to write what you hear Him saying to you. If you are new to this, ask the Holy Spirit to speak to you and teach you how to discern His Voice from all other voices. Write what you hear Him saying.

CHAPTER FOUR

Cataclysmic Transitions Throughout History

SCRIPTURES

1. **Ephesians 1:9-10**—*Having made known to us the mystery of His will, according to His good pleasure which He purposed in Himself,* [10] *that in* ***the dispensation of the fullness of the times*** *He might gather together in one all things in Christ, both which are in heaven and which are on earth—in Him.*

2. **First Corinthians 15:24-28**—*Then comes the end, when He delivers the kingdom to God the Father, when He puts an end to all rule and all authority and power.* [25] *For He must reign till He has put all enemies under His feet.* [26] *The last enemy that will be destroyed is death.* [27] *For "He has put all things under His feet." But when He says "all things are put under Him," it is evident that He who put all things under Him is excepted.* [28] *Now when all things are made subject to Him, then the Son Himself will also be subject to Him who put all things under Him, that God may be all in all.*

3. **First John 2:17**—*And* ***the world is passing away****, and the lust of it; but he who does the will of God abides forever.*

4. **First Corinthians 7:31 NIV**—*Those who use the things of the world, as if not engrossed in them. For* ***this world in its present form is passing away****.*

5. **Genesis 1:28–3:1-19**—*Due to the length of the text, please read from your Bible.*

6. **Genesis 2:16-17**—*And the LORD God commanded the man, saying, "Of every tree of the garden you may freely eat;* [17] *but of the tree of the knowledge of good and evil you shall not eat, for in the day that you eat of it you shall surely die."*

7. **Genesis 1:28**—*Then God blessed them, and God said to them, "Be fruitful and multiply; fill the earth and subdue it; have dominion over the fish of the sea, over the birds of the air, and over every living thing that moves on the earth."*

8. **Genesis 2:15**—*Then the LORD God took the man and put him in the garden of Eden to tend and keep it.*

9. **Genesis 3:1-6**—*Now the serpent was more cunning than any beast of the field which the LORD God had made. And he said to the woman, "Has God indeed said, 'You shall not eat of every tree of the garden'?" [2] And the woman said to the serpent, "We may eat the fruit of the trees of the garden; [3] but of the fruit of the tree which is in the midst of the garden, God has said, 'You shall not eat it, nor shall you touch it, lest you die.'" [4] Then the serpent said to the woman, "You will not surely die. [5] For God knows that in the day you eat of it your eyes will be opened, and you will be like God, knowing good and evil." [6] So when the woman saw that the tree was good for food, that it was pleasant to the eyes, and a tree desirable to make one wise, she took of its fruit and ate. She also gave to her husband with her, and he ate.*

10. **Genesis 3:14-24**— *So the LORD God said to the serpent: "Because you have done this, you are cursed more than all cattle, and more than every beast of the field; on your belly you shall go, and you shall eat dust all the days of your life. [15] And I will put enmity between you and the woman, and between your seed and her Seed; He shall bruise your head, and you shall bruise His heel." [16] To the woman He said: "I will greatly multiply your sorrow and your conception; in pain you shall bring forth children; your desire shall be for your husband, and he shall rule over you." [17] Then to Adam He said, "Because you have heeded the voice of your wife, and have eaten from the tree of which I commanded you, saying, 'You shall not eat of it': "Cursed is the ground for your sake; in toil you shall eat of it all the days of your life. [18] Both thorns and thistles it shall bring forth for you, and you shall eat the herb of the field. [19] In the sweat of your face you shall eat bread till you return to the ground, for out of it you were taken; for dust you are, and to dust you shall return." [20] And Adam called his wife's name Eve, because she was the mother of all living. [21] Also for Adam and his wife the LORD God made tunics of skin, and clothed them. [22] Then the LORD God said, "Behold, the man has become like one of Us, to know good and evil. And now, lest he put out his hand and take also of the tree of life, and eat, and live forever"— [23] therefore the LORD God sent him out of the garden of Eden to till the ground from which he was taken. [24] So He drove out the man; and He placed cherubim at the east of the garden of Eden, and a flaming sword which turned every way, to guard the way to the tree of life.*

11. **Genesis 3:23–8:19**—*Due to the length of the text, please read from your Bible.*

12. **Genesis 4:4**—*Abel also brought of the firstborn of his flock and of their fat. And the* LORD *respected Abel and his offering.*

13. **Genesis 4:7**—*If you do well, will you not be accepted? And if you do not do well, sin lies at the door. And its desire is for you, but you should rule over it.*

14. **Genesis 6:5, 11-12—***Then the* LORD *saw that the wickedness of man was great in the earth, and that every intent of the thoughts of his heart was only evil. ...* [11] *The earth also was corrupt before God, and the earth was filled with violence.* [12] *So God looked upon the earth, and indeed it was corrupt; for all flesh had corrupted their way on the earth.*

15. **Genesis 8:20-22–11:9**—*Due to the length of the text, please read from your Bible.*

16. **Genesis 9:5-6**—*Surely for your lifeblood I will demand a reckoning; from the hand of every beast I will require it, and from the hand of man. From the hand of every man's brother I will require the life of man.* [6] *"Whoever sheds man's blood, by man his blood shall be shed; for in the image of God He made man."*

17. **Genesis 9:1,7**—*So God blessed Noah and his sons, and said to them: "Be fruitful and multiply, and fill the earth. ...* [7] *And as for you, be fruitful and multiply; bring forth abundantly in the earth and multiply in it."*

18. **Genesis 11:1-4**—*Now the whole earth had one language and one speech.* [2] *And it came to pass, as they journeyed from the east, that they found a plain in the land of Shinar, and they dwelt there.* [3] *Then they said to one another, "Come, let us make bricks and bake them thoroughly." They had brick for stone, and they had asphalt for mortar.* [4] *And they said, "Come, let us build ourselves a city, and a tower whose top is in the heavens; let us make a name for ourselves, lest we be scattered abroad over the face of the whole earth."*

19. **Genesis 11:5-9**—*But the* LORD *came down to see the city and the tower which the sons of men had built.* [6] *And the* LORD *said, "Indeed the people are one and they all have one language, and this is what they begin to do; now nothing that they propose to do will be withheld from them.* [7] *Come, let Us go down and there confuse their language, that they may not understand one another's speech."* [8] *So the* LORD *scattered them abroad from there over the face of all the earth, and they ceased building the city.* [9] *Therefore its name is called Babel, because there the* LORD *confused the language of all the earth; and from there the* LORD *scattered them abroad over the face of all the earth.*

20. **Genesis 11:10–Exodus 19:4**—*Due to the length of the text, please read from your Bible.*

21. **Genesis 12:1-3**—*Now the LORD had said to Abram: "Get out of your country, from your family and from your father's house, to a land that I will show you. [2] I will make you a great nation; I will bless you and make your name great; and you shall be a blessing. [3] I will bless those who bless you, and I will curse him who curses you; and in you all the families of the earth shall be blessed."*

22. **Genesis 15:6**—*And he believed in the LORD, and He accounted it to him for righteousness.*

23. **Genesis 17:1**—*When Abram was ninety-nine years old, the LORD appeared to Abram and said to him, "I am Almighty God; walk before Me and be blameless."*

24. **Hebrews 11:8-10**—*By faith Abraham obeyed when he was called to go out to the place which he would receive as an inheritance. And he went out, not knowing where he was going. [9] By faith he dwelt in the land of promise as in a foreign country, dwelling in tents with Isaac and Jacob, the heirs with him of the same promise; [10] for he waited for the city which has foundations, whose builder and maker is God.*

25. **Genesis 37**—*Due to the length of the text, please read from your Bible.*

26. **Exodus 1-19**—*Due to the length of the text, please read from your Bible.*

27. **Exodus 19:5–John 19:30**—*Due to the length of the text, please read from your Bible.*

28. **Exodus 20:1-17**—*And God spoke all these words, saying: [2] "I am the LORD your God, who brought you out of the land of Egypt, out of the house of bondage. [3] You shall have no other gods before Me. [4] You shall not make for yourself a carved image—any likeness of anything that is in heaven above, or that is in the earth beneath, or that is in the water under the earth; [5] you shall not bow down to them nor serve them. For I, the LORD your God, am a jealous God, visiting the iniquity of the fathers upon the children to the third and fourth generations of those who hate Me, [6] but showing mercy to thousands, to those who love Me and keep My commandments. [7] You shall not take the name of the LORD your God in vain, for the LORD will not hold him guiltless who takes His name in vain. [8] Remember the Sabbath day, to keep it holy. [9] Six days you shall labor and do all your work, [10] but the seventh day is the Sabbath of the LORD your God. In it you shall do no work: you, nor your son, nor your daughter, nor your male servant, nor your female servant, nor your cattle, nor your stranger who is within your gates. [11] For in six days the LORD made the heavens and the earth, the sea, and all that is in them, and rested the seventh day. Therefore the LORD blessed the Sabbath day and hallowed it. [12] Honor your father and your mother, that your days may be long upon the*

land which the L*ORD your God is giving you.* [13] *You shall not murder.* [14] *You shall not commit adultery.* [15] *You shall not steal.* [16] *You shall not bear false witness against your neighbor.* [17] *You shall not covet your neighbor's house; you shall not covet your neighbor's wife, nor his male servant, nor his female servant, nor his ox, nor his donkey, nor anything that is your neighbor's."*

29. **Deuteronomy 28**—*Due to the length of the text, please read from your Bible.*

30. **Leviticus 1–7**—*Due to the length of the text, please read from your Bible.*

31. **Matthew 27**—*Due to the length of the text, please read from your Bible.*

32. **Hebrews 10:1-18**—*For the law, having a shadow of the good things to come, and not the very image of the things, can never with these same sacrifices, which they offer continually year by year, make those who approach perfect.* [2] *For then would they not have ceased to be offered? For the worshipers, once purified, would have had no more consciousness of sins.* [3] *But in those sacrifices there is a reminder of sins every year.* [4] *For it is not possible that the blood of bulls and goats could take away sins.* [5] *Therefore, when He came into the world, He said: "Sacrifice and offering You did not desire, but a body You have prepared for Me.* [6] *In burnt offerings and sacrifices for sinYou had no pleasure.* [7] *Then I said, 'Behold, I have come— In the volume of the book it is written of Me—to do Your will, O God.'"* [8] *Previously saying, "Sacrifice and offering, burnt offerings, and offerings for sin You did not desire, nor had pleasure in them" (which are offered according to the law),* [9] *then He said, "Behold, I have come to do Your will, O God." He takes away the first that He may establish the second.* [10] *By that will we have been sanctified through the offering of the body of Jesus Christ once for all.* [11] *And every priest stands ministering daily and offering repeatedly the same sacrifices, which can never take away sins.* [12] *But this Man, after He had offered one sacrifice for sins forever, sat down at the right hand of God,* [13] *from that time waiting till His enemies are made His footstool.* [14] *For by one offering He has perfected forever those who are being sanctified.* [15] *But the Holy Spirit also witnesses to us; for after He had said before,* [16] *"This is the covenant that I will make with them after those days, says the* L*ORD: I will put My laws into their hearts, and in their minds I will write them,"* [17] *then He adds, "Their sins and their lawless deeds I will remember no more."* [18] *Now where there is remission of these, there is no longer an offering for sin.*

33. **John 19:31–Revelation 3:22**—*Due to the length of the text, please read from your Bible.*

34. **Ephesians 2:8-9**—*For by grace you have been saved through faith, and that not of yourselves; it is the gift of God,* [9] *not of works, lest anyone should boast.*

35. **Matthew 28:19-20**—*Go therefore and make disciples of all the nations, baptizing them in the name of the Father and of the Son and of the Holy Spirit, [20] teaching them to observe all things that I have commanded you; and lo, I am with you always, even to the end of the age. Amen.*

36. **Galatians 5:16**—*I say then: Walk in the Spirit, and you shall not fulfill the lust of the flesh.*

37. **John 13:34-35**—*A new commandment I give to you, that you love one another; as I have loved you, that you also love one another. [35] By this all will know that you are My disciples, if you have love for one another.*

38. **Second Timothy 3:1-5**—*But know this, that in the last days perilous times will come: [2] For men will be lovers of themselves, lovers of money, boasters, proud, blasphemers, disobedient to parents, unthankful, unholy, [3] unloving, unforgiving, slanderers, without self-control, brutal, despisers of good, [4] traitors, headstrong, haughty, lovers of pleasure rather than lovers of God, [5] having a form of godliness but denying its power. And from such people turn away!*

39. **Revelation 2–3**—*Due to the length of the text, please read from your Bible.*

40. **First Thessalonians 4:16-17**—*For the Lord Himself will descend from heaven with a shout, with the voice of an archangel, and with the trumpet of God. And the dead in Christ will rise first. [17] Then we who are alive and remain shall be caught up together with them in the clouds to meet the Lord in the air. And thus we shall always be with the Lord.*

41. **Revelation 20:1-10**—*Then I saw an angel coming down from heaven, having the key to the bottomless pit and a great chain in his hand. [2] He laid hold of the dragon, that serpent of old, who is the Devil and Satan, and bound him for a thousand years; [3] and he cast him into the bottomless pit, and shut him up, and set a seal on him, so that he should deceive the nations no more till the thousand years were finished. But after these things he must be released for a little while. [4] And I saw thrones, and they sat on them, and judgment was committed to them. Then I saw the souls of those who had been beheaded for their witness to Jesus and for the word of God, who had not worshiped the beast or his image, and had not received his mark on their foreheads or on their hands. And they lived and reigned with Christ for a thousand years. [5] But the rest of the dead did not live again until the thousand years were finished. This is the first resurrection. [6] Blessed and holy is he who has part in the first resurrection. Over such the second death has no power, but they shall be priests of God and of Christ, and shall reign with Him a thousand years. [7] Now when the thousand years have expired, Satan will be*

released from his prison [8] and will go out to deceive the nations which are in the four corners of the earth, Gog and Magog, to gather them together to battle, whose number is as the sand of the sea. [9] They went up on the breadth of the earth and surrounded the camp of the saints and the beloved city. And fire came down from God out of heaven and devoured them. [10] The devil, who deceived them, was cast into the lake of fire and brimstone where the beast and the false prophet are. And they will be tormented day and night forever and ever.

42. **Isaiah 11:1-9**—*There shall come forth a Rod from the stem of Jesse, and a Branch shall grow out of his roots. [2] The Spirit of the LORD shall rest upon Him, the Spirit of wisdom and understanding, the Spirit of counsel and might, the Spirit of knowledge and of the fear of the LORD. [3] His delight is in the fear of the LORD, and He shall not judge by the sight of His eyes, nor decide by the hearing of His ears; [4] but with righteousness He shall judge the poor, and decide with equity for the meek of the earth; He shall strike the earth with the rod of His mouth, and with the breath of His lips He shall slay the wicked. [5] Righteousness shall be the belt of His loins, and faithfulness the belt of His waist. [6] The wolf also shall dwell with the lamb, the leopard shall lie down with the young goat, the calf and the young lion and the fatling together; and a little child shall lead them. [7] The cow and the bear shall graze; their young ones shall lie down together; and the lion shall eat straw like the ox. [8] The nursing child shall play by the cobra's hole, and the weaned child shall put his hand in the viper's den. [9] They shall not hurt nor destroy in all My holy mountain, for the earth shall be full of the knowledge of the LORD as the waters cover the sea.*

43. **Zechariah 14:16-19**—*And it shall come to pass that everyone who is left of all the nations which came against Jerusalem shall go up from year to year to worship the King, the LORD of hosts, and to keep the Feast of Tabernacles. [17] And it shall be that whichever of the families of the earth do not come up to Jerusalem to worship the King, the LORD of hosts, on them there will be no rain. [18] If the family of Egypt will not come up and enter in, they shall have no rain; they shall receive the plague with which the LORD strikes the nations who do not come up to keep the Feast of Tabernacles. [19] This shall be the punishment of Egypt and the punishment of all the nations that do not come up to keep the Feast of Tabernacles.*

44. **Revelation 20:11-15**—*Then I saw a great white throne and Him who sat on it, from whose face the earth and the heaven fled away. And there was found no place for them. [12] And I saw the dead, small and great, standing before God, and books were opened. And another book was opened, which is the Book of Life. And the dead were judged according to their works, by the things which were written in the books. [13] The sea gave up the dead who were in it, and Death and Hades delivered up the dead who were in them. And they were judged, each*

one according to his works. [14] Then Death and Hades were cast into the lake of fire. This is the second death. [15] And anyone not found written in the Book of Life was cast into the lake of fire.

45. **Revelation 21:1**—*Now I saw a new heaven and a new earth, for the first heaven and the first earth had passed away. Also there was no more sea.*

46. **Revelation 22:5**—*There shall be no night there: They need no lamp nor light of the sun, for the Lord God gives them light. And they shall reign forever and ever.*

47. **Matthew 24:3-14**—*Now as He sat on the Mount of Olives, the disciples came to Him privately, saying, "Tell us, when will these things be? And what will be the sign of Your coming, and of the end of the age?" [4] And Jesus answered and said to them: "Take heed that no one deceives you. [5] For many will come in My name, saying, 'I am the Christ,' and will deceive many. [6] And you will hear of wars and rumors of wars. See that you are not troubled; for all these things must come to pass, but the end is not yet. [7] For nation will rise against nation, and kingdom against kingdom. And there will be famines, pestilences, and earthquakes in various places. [8] All these are the beginning of sorrows. [9] "Then they will deliver you up to tribulation and kill you, and you will be hated by all nations for My name's sake. [10] And then many will be offended, will betray one another, and will hate one another. [11] Then many false prophets will rise up and deceive many. [12] And because lawlessness will abound, the love of many will grow cold. [13] But he who endures to the end shall be saved. [14] And this gospel of the kingdom will be preached in all the world as a witness to all the nations, and then the end will come."*

48. **Hebrews 1:10-12**—*And: "You, LORD, in the beginning laid the foundation of the earth, and the heavens are the work of Your hands. [11] They will perish, but You remain; and they will all grow old like a garment; [12] like a cloak You will fold them up, and they will be changed. But You are the same, and Your years will not fail."*

49. **Hebrews 1:1-2**—*God, who at various times and in various ways spoke in time past to the fathers by the prophets, [2] has in these last days spoken to us by His Son, whom He has appointed heir of all things, through whom also He made the worlds.*

50. **Matthew 12:32**—*Anyone who speaks a word against the Son of Man, it will be forgiven him; but whoever speaks against the Holy Spirit, it will not be forgiven him, either in this age or in the **age** to come.*

51. **Matthew 13:39**—*The enemy who sowed them is the devil, the harvest is the end of the **age**, and the reapers are the angels.*

52. **Ephesians 2:7**—*That in the **ages** to come He might show the exceeding riches of His grace in His kindness toward us in Christ Jesus.*

53. **Colossians 1:26**—*The mystery which has been hidden from **ages** and from generations, but now has been revealed to His saints.*

54. **Ephesians 2:2**—*In which you once walked according to the course of this **world**, according to the prince of the power of the air, the spirit who now works in the sons of disobedience.*

55. **Isaiah 9:6**—*For unto us a Child is born, unto us a Son is given; and the government will be upon His shoulder. And His name will be called Wonderful, Counselor, Mighty God, Everlasting Father, Prince of Peace.*

56. **John 1:3**—***All things were made through Him,*** *and without Him nothing was made that was made.*

57. **Colossians 1:15-18**—*He is the image of the invisible God, the firstborn over all creation.* [16] ***For by Him all things were created*** *that are in heaven and that are on earth, visible and invisible, whether thrones or dominions or principalities or powers. All things were created through Him and for Him.* [17] *And He is before all things, and in Him all things consist.* [18] *And He is the head of the body, the church, who is the beginning, the firstborn from the dead, that in all things He may have the preeminence.*

58. **Ephesians 3:9**—*And to make all see what is the fellowship of the mystery, which from the beginning of the ages has been hidden in God **who created all things through Jesus Christ.***

59. **Genesis 49:1**—*And Jacob called his sons and said, "Gather together, that I may tell you what shall befall you in the **last days**."*

60. **Acts 2:17**—*And it shall come to pass in the **last days**, says God, that I will pour out of My Spirit on all flesh; your sons and your daughters shall prophesy, your young men shall see visions, your old men shall dream dreams.*

61. **Second Timothy 3:1**—*But know this, that in the **last days** perilous times will come.*

62. **Deuteronomy 4:30**—*When you are in distress, and all these things come upon you in the **latter days,** when you turn to the LORD your God and obey His voice.*

63. **Deuteronomy 31:29**—*For I know that after my death you will become utterly corrupt, and turn aside from the way which I have commanded you. And evil will befall you in the* ***latter days****, because you will do evil in the sight of the* L*ORD*, *to provoke Him to anger through the work of your hands.*

64. **Isaiah 2:2**—*Now it shall come to pass in the* ***latter days*** *that the mountain of the* L*ORD's house shall be established on the top of the mountains, and shall be exalted above the hills; and all nations shall flow to it.*

65. **Daniel 2:28**—*But there is a God in heaven who reveals secrets, and He has made known to King Nebuchadnezzar what will be in the* ***latter days****. Your dream, and the visions of your head upon your bed, were these.*

66. **Daniel 10:14**—*Now I have come to make you understand what will happen to your people in the* ***latter days****, for the vision refers to many days yet to come.*

67. **Daniel 8:17**—*So he came near where I stood, and when he came I was afraid and fell on my face; but he said to me, "Understand, son of man, that the vision refers to the* ***time of the end****."*

68. **Daniel 11:35**—*And some of those understanding shall fall, to refine them, purify them, and make them white, until the* ***time of the end****; because it is still for the appointed time.*

69. **Daniel 12:4, 9**—*"But you, Daniel, shut up the words, and seal the book until the* ***time of the end****; many shall run to and fro, and knowledge shall increase." ... [9] And he said, "Go your way, Daniel, for the words are closed up and sealed till the* ***time of the end****."*

70. **Job 19:25**—*For I know that my Redeemer lives, and He shall stand* ***at last*** *on the earth.*

71. **Daniel 12:13**—*But you, go your way till the end; for you shall rest, and will arise to your inheritance at the* ***end of the days****.*

72. **Isaiah 2:12**—*For the* ***day of the Lord*** *of hosts shall come upon everything proud and lofty, upon everything lifted up—and it shall be brought low.*

73. **Isaiah 13:6**—*Wail, for the* ***day of the Lord*** *is at hand! It will come as destruction from the Almighty.*

74. **Joel 1:15**—*Alas for the day! For the* ***day of the Lord*** *is at hand; it shall come as destruction from the Almighty.*

75. **Joel 2:1**—*Blow the trumpet in Zion, and sound an alarm in My holy mountain! Let all the inhabitants of the land tremble; for the* ***day of the Lord*** *is coming, for it is at hand.*

76. **Malachi 4:5**—*Behold, I will send you Elijah the prophet before the coming of the great and dreadful* ***day of the Lord****.*

77. **First Thessalonians 5:2**—*For you yourselves know perfectly that the* ***day of the Lord*** *so comes as a thief in the night.*

78. **Second Peter 3:10**—*But the* ***day of the Lord*** *will come as a thief in the night, in which the heavens will pass away with a great noise, and the elements will melt with fervent heat; both the earth and the works that are in it will be burned up.*

79. **Isaiah 2:11**—*The lofty looks of man shall be humbled, the haughtiness of men shall be bowed down, and the* LORD *alone shall be exalted in* ***that day****.*

80. **Isaiah 4:1**—*And in* ***that day*** *seven women shall take hold of one man, saying, "We will eat our own food and wear our own apparel; only let us be called by your name, to take away our reproach."*

81. **Zechariah 14:4**—*And in* ***that day*** *His feet will stand on the Mount of Olives, which faces Jerusalem on the east. And the Mount of Olives shall be split in two, from east to west, making a very large valley; half of the mountain shall move toward the north and half of it toward the south.*

82. **First Peter 1:5, 20**—*who are kept by the power of God through faith for salvation ready to be revealed in the* ***last time.*** *… [20] He indeed was foreordained before the foundation of the world, but was manifest in these* ***last times*** *for you.*

83. **Jude 1:18**—*How they told you that there would be mockers in the* ***last time*** *who would walk according to their own ungodly lusts.*

84. **First John 2:18**—*Little children, it is the last hour; and as you have heard that the Antichrist is coming, even now many antichrists have come, by which we know that it is the last hour.*

85. **Daniel 2:44**—*And in the days of these kings the God of heaven will set up a kingdom which shall never be destroyed; and the kingdom shall not be left to other people; it shall break in pieces and consume all these kingdoms, and it shall stand forever.*

86. **Matthew 28:20**—*"Teaching them to observe all things that I have commanded you; and lo, I am with you always, even to the* ***end of the age****." Amen.*

87. **Hebrews 9:26**—*He then would have had to suffer often since the foundation of the world; but now, once at the* ***end of the ages****, He has appeared to put away sin by the sacrifice of Himself.*

88. **Ezekiel 38:16**—*You will come up against My people Israel like a cloud, to cover the land. It will be in the* ***latter days*** *that I will bring you against My land, so that the nations may know Me, when I am hallowed in you, O Gog, before their eyes.*

89. **First Timothy 4:1**—*Now the Spirit expressly says that in* ***latter times*** *some will depart from the faith, giving heed to deceiving spirits and doctrines of demons.*

90. **Daniel 12:8**—*Although I heard, I did not understand. Then I said, "My lord, what shall be* ***the end*** *of these things?"*

91. **Matthew 24:3, 14**—*Now as He sat on the Mount of Olives, the disciples came to Him privately, saying, "Tell us, when will these things be? And what will be the sign of Your coming, and of* ***the end*** *of the age?" ...* [14] *"And this gospel of the kingdom will be preached in all the world as a witness to all the nations, and then* ***the end*** *will come."*

92. **Jeremiah 30:7**—*Alas! For that day is great, so that none is like it; and it is the* ***time of Jacob's trouble****, but he shall be saved out of it.*

93. **Daniel 12:1**—*At that time Michael shall stand up, the great prince who stands watch over the sons of your people; and there shall be a* ***time of trouble****, such as never was since there was a nation, even to that time. And at that time your people shall be delivered, every one who is found written in the book.*

94. **Matthew 24:21**—*For then there will be great tribulation, such as has not been since the beginning of the world until this time, no, nor ever shall be.*

95. **Joel 1:15**—*Alas for the day! For* ***the day*** *of the LORD is at hand; it shall come as destruction from the Almighty.*

96. **Zephaniah 1:7**—*Be silent in the presence of the Lord GOD; for* ***the day*** *of the LORD is at hand, for the LORD has prepared a sacrifice; He has invited His guests.*

97. **Zechariah 14:1**—*Behold,* ***the day*** *of the LORD is coming, and your spoil will be divided in your midst.*

98. **Hebrews 1:2-3**—*Has in these* ***last days*** *spoken to us by His Son, whom He has appointed heir of all things, through whom also He made the worlds;* [3] *who being the brightness of His glory and the express image of His person, and upholding all things by the word of His power, when He had by Himself purged our sins, sat down at the right hand of the Majesty on high.*

99. **Romans 8:17-19**—*And if children, then heirs—heirs of God* ***and joint heirs with Christ****, if indeed we suffer with Him, that we may also be glorified together.* [18] *For I consider that the sufferings of this present time are not worthy to be compared with the glory which shall be revealed in us.* [19] *For the earnest expectation of the creation eagerly waits for the revealing of the sons of God.*

100. **Hebrews 12:3-4**—*For consider Him who endured such hostility from sinners against Himself, lest you become weary and discouraged in your souls.* [4] *You have not yet resisted to bloodshed, striving against sin.*

101. **Acts 26:18**—*To open their eyes, in order to turn them from darkness to light, and from the power of Satan to God, that they may receive forgiveness of sins and an* ***inheritance*** *among those who are sanctified by faith in Me.*

102. **First Peter 1:4-5**—*To an* ***inheritance*** *incorruptible and undefiled and that does not fade away, reserved in heaven for you,* [5] *who are kept by the power of God through faith for salvation ready to be revealed in the last time.*

THE FULLNESS OF TIMES

God will bring His eternal plan to completion by uniting all things—heavenly and earthly—under Jesus Christ's leadership, fulfilling His goal to restore creation's harmony. This marks the conclusion of previous ages and the beginning of God's ultimate, unified rule centered on Christ.

SEGMENTS OF TIME AND TEMPORARY KINGDOMS ALLOTTED FOR MANKIND

Life can be here in one instance, and the very next moment can be gone, leaving someone to face eternity, whether in heaven or hell. The term "passing away" signifies that what we do now could pass away into the next life. What steps can you take to ensure that you make the most of your time here to prepare for your time there?

PREVIOUS AGES, OR DISPENSATIONS, EACH ENDING WITH A CATACLYSMIC BANG!

FOCUS POINT

We are in the Age of Grace, which began on the day of Pentecost, when the believers were filled with the Holy Spirit in Acts 2. Since then, the gospel has spread around the world. This is an incredible feat that could only happen with the help of the Holy Spirit and willing vessels ready to carry the message of Jesus to a lost and dying world. Salvation became available to everyone, and the message of grace through faith spread rapidly. Even though there has been so much evil throughout the generations, what Jesus did when He died on the cross shows that we are more than conquerors and can overcome everything the enemy throws our way. Take this time to thank Jesus for the message of grace and for salvation that comes through what He did on the cross, not by works. Write Ephesians 2:8-9 on the lines provided.

LIST OF BIRTH PANGS

The list of birth pangs reveals what will happen when the end is near. Looking at the birth pangs, what signs are already taking place in the world? How are you preparing for Jesus' return?

JESUS MADE THE WORLD, ALSO KNOWN AS AGES AND DISPENSATIONS

God has been speaking to us through Jesus throughout the ages. The Father used the Son to save the world and to make a way back to the Father. Without Jesus, we would not have access to God. A world that was once dying and on its way to an eternity separated from God was given the best gift of salvation, a forever future with the Creator of all things, and the status of heirs with Jesus.

ALL THINGS WERE MADE THROUGH JESUS.

Creation was made through Jesus. John 1:3 says, *"All things were made through Him, and without Him nothing was made that was made."* This means that if Jesus weren't here, nothing would have ever been made. With this understanding, what are your thoughts on the importance of Jesus and creation?

FOURTEEN BIBLICAL EXPRESSIONS RELATING TO THE LAST DAYS

Throughout Scripture, countless prophecies speak of the end times, or last days. God has been preparing the way for Jesus' return for the Church since the very beginning. Lucifer's rebellion and Adam and Eve's sin created the need for a Savior and for these prophecies. After reviewing the list of biblical expressions, how do the various terms—such as "last days," "latter days," "time of the end," and "day of the Lord"—shape your understanding of God's prophetic timeline and the role of believers in these times?

EIGHT BIBLICAL TRUTHS ABOUT JESUS CHRIST AS THEY RELATE TO THE LAST DAYS

Hebrews 1:2-3 describes Jesus in eight different ways. How do these attributes of Jesus help you understand His role in God's plan for humanity and your personal faith journey?

BELIEVERS ARE HEIRS OF ALL THINGS

Romans 8:17 says that believers are "heirs of God and joint heirs with Christ." What does it mean to you to be a joint heir with Christ?

JOINT HEIRS IF INDEED WE SUFFER WITH HIM

Romans 8:18 continues, stating that "the sufferings of this present time are not worthy to be compared with the glory that will be revealed in us." How does this promise of future glory affect your perspective on present challenges?

What does it mean to "suffer with Christ" in the context of resisting sin, and how does that perspective influence the way you approach challenges and temptations in your daily life?

THE PROMISE OF AN ETERNAL INHERITANCE

PERSONAL REFLECTIONS

As believers, being joint heirs with Christ means our present sufferings and challenges are not the end of the story. Instead, they are part of a journey toward a future glory and inheritance that far outweighs anything we face now. This promise encourages us to persevere, knowing that God has prepared something extraordinary for those who remain faithful.

Take this time to thank God that you are a joint heir with Jesus. Ask Him to help you through everything that is happening in your life and in the world around you. Write down your prayer and what you hear Him say.

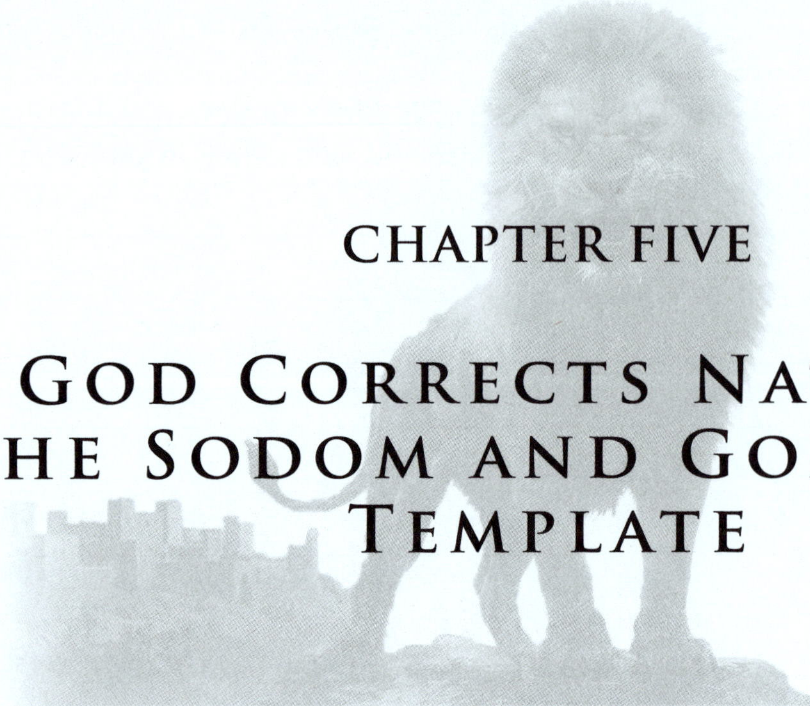

CHAPTER FIVE

GOD CORRECTS NATIONS: THE SODOM AND GOMORRAH TEMPLATE

SCRIPTURES

1. **Psalm 2:1-5**—*Why do the nations rage, and the people plot a vain thing? [2] The kings of the earth set themselves, and the rulers take counsel together, against the LORD and against His Anointed, saying, [3] "Let us break Their bonds in pieces and cast away Their cords from us." [4] He who sits in the heavens shall laugh; the LORD shall hold them in derision. [5] Then He shall speak to them in His wrath, and distress them in His deep displeasure.*

2. **Luke 1:17**—*He will also go before Him in the spirit and power of Elijah, "**to turn the hearts of the fathers to the children**," and the disobedient to the wisdom of the just, to make ready a people prepared for the Lord.*

3. **Matthew 7:13-14**—*Enter by the narrow gate; for wide is the gate and broad is the way that leads to destruction, and there are many who go in by it. [14] Because narrow is the gate and difficult is the way which leads to life, and there are few who find it.*

4. **Genesis 18:21**—*I will go down now and see whether they have done altogether according to the outcry against it that has come to Me; and if not, I will know.*

5. **Genesis 19:13**—*For we will destroy this place, because the outcry against them has grown great before the face of the LORD, and the LORD has sent us to destroy it.*

6. **Genesis 19:24-25**—*Then the LORD rained brimstone and fire on Sodom and Gomorrah, from the LORD out of the heavens. [25] So He overthrew those cities, all the plain, all the inhabitants of the cities, and what grew on the ground.*

7. **Isaiah 3:9**—*The look on their countenance witnesses against them, and they declare their sin as Sodom; they do not hide it. Woe to their soul! For they have brought evil upon themselves.*

8. **Genesis 18:19**—*For I have known him, in order that he may command his children and his household after him, that they keep the way of the LORD, to do righteousness and justice, that the LORD may bring to Abraham what He has spoken to him.*

9. **Psalm 25:12-14**—*Who is the man that fears the LORD? Him shall He teach in the way He chooses.* [13] *He himself shall dwell in prosperity, and his descendants shall inherit the earth.* [14] ***The secret of the LORD is with those who fear Him, and He will show them His covenant.***

10. **Galatians 6:7**—*Do not be deceived, God is not mocked; for whatever a man sows, that he will also reap.*

11. **Acts 12:21-23**—*So on a set day Herod, arrayed in royal apparel, sat on his throne and gave an oration to them.* [22] *And the people kept shouting, "The voice of a god and not of a man!"* [23] *Then immediately an angel of the Lord struck him, because he did not give glory to God. And he was eaten by worms and died.*

12. **Matthew 24:21**—*For then there will be great tribulation, such as has not been since the beginning of the world until this time, no, nor ever shall be.*

For those who are part of the Church, it is hard to imagine why anyone, or any nation, would align themselves with an Antichrist system, yet we see it on display in the culture and in geopolitics. As believers, we know the truth of God's Word, His promises, and what He provides for His children. How is it possible that so many are deceived into following the enemy's lies? Read John 10:10 and write the difference between what Satan does and what Jesus does.

____

____

____

____

____

____

GOD DEALS WITH INDIVIDUALS DIFFERENTLY FROM NATIONS

Second Peter 3:9 says, *"The Lord is not slack concerning His promise, as some count slackness, but is longsuffering toward us, not willing that any should perish but that all should come to repentance."* Knowing that God deals with individuals differently from nations, how does this scripture show God's patience toward humanity and His reasoning for discipline?

____

____

____

____

____

____

REVIVAL PRECEDES REFORMATION

Look up the word "reformed" in your dictionary. Write the definition on the lines provided, and then describe what it looks like for a nation to experience revival and reformation based on the definition.

____

____

____

____

____

____

DISOBEDIENT TURNED TO THE WISDOM OF THE JUST

FOCUS POINT

Luke 1:17 says, *"and the **disobedient** to the wisdom of the just, to make ready a people prepared for the Lord."*

From *Gill's Exposition of the Whole Bible*: "By the 'disobedient' are meant, either Jews or Gentiles; some understand it of the Gentiles, who were children of disobedience, before the light of the gospel came among them: but rather the former are meant, who were a disobedient, rebellious, and gainsaying people; who were gone off from the wisdom, knowledge, and religion, of the just, or righteous ones, their forefathers; who prophesied of Christ, rejoiced to see his day, longed for him, and believed in him: now John was to be an instrument of turning some of the unbelieving Jews, to the true knowledge of salvation by Christ; which their righteous progenitors waited for, had a right knowledge of, and an interest in: and of leading them either into the gospel of Christ, that wisdom of God is a mystery; the manifold wisdom of God, in which he has abounded in all wisdom and prudence: and which the righteous men among the Jews, searched diligently into, attained some knowledge of, and which even the holy angels desire to look into; so the patriarchs were called just, or righteous; as righteous Abel, just Noah and so the Jewish fathers."[1]

The disobedient are those unaware of Jesus and the gospel. The just are the righteous. When the righteous are the dominant influence in a society, even the disobedient come under their persuasion, making society a much better place. With this understanding, the righteous are called to minister the truth of the gospel and of Jesus to a lost and dying world, also known as the disobedient. Be a light today and share with those around you.

GOD DEALT WITH NATIONS THROUGHOUT THE OLD TESTAMENT, AND HE CONTINUES THIS TODAY

God judges individuals based on their personal relationship with Jesus Christ, not on the actions of their nation or church. Given this, how can you actively be "salt and light" in your community, even if the nation or church you belong to is not following God's principles?

____

____

____

THE SODOM AND GOMORRAH TEMPLATE

It is unclear who was crying out to God about the evil taking place in Sodom and Gomorrah. It could have been Lot and his family, innocent people who were victimized, or even those committing the vile acts. If it were those who participated in the acts, it would reveal that even the lost can cry out in a way that reaches heaven. It doesn't mean they believe in God or even want to change. But it does mean they are aware of the darkness and what it produces.

ANGELIC VISITORS ON ASSIGNMENT TO DESTROY SODOM AND GOMORRAH

God was aware of what was taking place in Sodom and Gomorrah. He heard the cries of the people and responded with severe judgment. Even through this type of punishment, what does it reveal about God's character when He takes a stand against evil?

LOT'S FOOLISH DECISION TO DWELL IN SODOM AND GOMORRAH

Lot chose to reside in these evil cities. According to Genesis 13:10, these places were "well-watered' and compared to "the garden of the Lord." Sometimes people make decisions based on a few factors rather than the whole picture. In this situation, Lot was drawn by the location's resources rather than the evil taking place. When making a decision, make sure to examine everything and be led by the Holy Spirit. God desires to direct your path. Read Proverbs 3:5-6. Write it out on the lines provided.

____

____

____

____

____

____

WHAT CAUSED THE LORD TO SHARE HIS PLAN FOR SODOM AND GOMORRAH WITH ABRAHAM?

Of the three reasons God decided to reveal His plan to Abraham, which one stands out most to you? Can you apply that one to your life? If so, why or why not?

____

____

____

____

____

____

GOD'S COVENANT WITH ABRAHAM CAUSED GOD TO SHARE HIS SECRET

God desires to show His covenant to those who fear Him. What is the difference between fearing the Lord and being afraid of Him? How does this understanding reveal who God will show His covenant to?

____

____

____

____

WHEN PUSHED, GOD WILL RIGHTSIZE WICKEDNESS

The concept of sowing and reaping appears in many areas of someone's life. In the situations listed in this section, what did they sow and what did they reap?

Tower of Babel:

Nineveh:

The Philistine Army and Goliath:

REAPING THE JUDGMENT OF GOD IS NOT EXCLUSIVE TO THE OLD TESTAMENT: HEROD EATEN BY WORMS

Even though King Herod knew he wasn't a god, he never denied it. According to Josephus, Herod acknowledged that he was dying. Once a proud man, he was humbled to the point of weeping on the floor. Pride has a way of blinding someone to the truth or keeping someone from speaking up about what is true. Like Satan, who believed he could be like God, King Herod not only believed but also agreed with what people were saying about him. This changed when he realized his health was failing.

IF SCHOOLS DESIRE TO TEACH THE HISTORY OF SEXUAL PERVERSION THEY SHOULD START WITH SODOM AND GOMORRAH

PERSONAL REFLECTIONS

We are living in a culture that is pushing a perverse agenda and growing increasingly similar to Sodom and Gomorrah. What should we do about this? Believers are called to be a source of hope and transformation. The gospel of Jesus Christ is the answer that can rescue individuals and entire cultures from judgment and despair. Each believer has a unique role to play as an agent of change, empowered to bring light into darkness and to stand in the gap for those around them. How can you be this light and stand in the gap for those around you? Take this time to write your answer and spend time with Jesus, asking Him to help and guide you.

CHAPTER SIX

Josiah and Cyrus: Agents of National Reformation

SCRIPTURES

1. **First Kings 13:1-2**—*And behold, a man of God went from Judah to Bethel by the word of the LORD, and Jeroboam stood by the altar to burn incense. 2 Then he cried out against the altar by the word of the LORD, and said, "O altar, altar! Thus says the LORD: 'Behold, a child, Josiah by name, shall be born to the house of David; and on you he shall sacrifice the priests of the high places who burn incense on you, and men's bones shall be burned on you.'"*

2. **Second Kings 22:1**—*Josiah was eight years old when he became king, and he reigned thirty-one years in Jerusalem. His mother's name was Jedidah the daughter of Adaiah of Bozkath.*

3. **Second Kings 22:3, 8-11**—*Now it came to pass, in the eighteenth year of King Josiah, that the king sent Shaphan the scribe, the son of Azaliah, the son of Meshullam, to the house of the LORD. 8 ...Then Hilkiah the high priest said to Shaphan the scribe, "I have found the Book of the Law in the house of the LORD." And Hilkiah gave the book to Shaphan, and he read it. 9 So Shaphan the scribe went to the king, bringing the king word, saying, "Your servants have gathered the money that was found in the house, and have delivered it into the hand of those who do the work, who oversee the house of the LORD." 10 Then Shaphan the scribe showed the king, saying, "Hilkiah the priest has given me a book." And Shaphan read it before the king. 11 Now it happened, when the king heard the words of the Book of the Law, that he tore his clothes.*

4. **Ephesians 1:5**—*Having predestined us to adoption as sons by Jesus Christ to Himself, according to the good pleasure of His will.*

5. **Romans 14:17**—*For the kingdom of God is not eating and drinking, but righteousness and peace and joy in the Holy Spirit.*

6. **Second Kings 22:18-20**—*But as for the king of Judah, who sent you to inquire of the LORD, in this manner you shall speak to him, "Thus says the LORD God of Israel: 'Concerning the words which you have heard—* [19] *because your heart was tender, and you humbled yourself before the LORD when you heard what I spoke against this place and against its inhabitants, that they would become a desolation and a curse, and you tore your clothes and wept before Me, I also have heard you,' says the LORD.* [20] *'Surely, therefore, I will gather you to your fathers, and you shall be gathered to your grave in peace; and your eyes shall not see all the calamity which I will bring on this place.'" So they brought back word to the king.*

7. **Second Kings 23:24-27**—*Moreover Josiah put away those who consulted mediums and spiritists, the household gods and idols, all the abominations that were seen in the land of Judah and in Jerusalem, that he might perform the words of the law which were written in the book that Hilkiah the priest found in the house of the LORD.* [25] *Now before him there was no king like him, who turned to the LORD with all his heart, with all his soul, and with all his might, according to all the Law of Moses; nor after him did any arise like him.* [26] *Nevertheless the LORD did not turn from the fierceness of His great wrath, with which His anger was aroused against Judah, because of all the provocations with which Manasseh had provoked Him.* [27] *And the LORD said, "I will also remove Judah from My sight, as I have removed Israel, and will cast off this city Jerusalem which I have chosen, and the house of which I said, 'My name shall be there.'"*

8. **Second Kings 23:29-30**—*In his days Pharaoh Necho king of Egypt went to the aid of the king of Assyria, to the River Euphrates; and King Josiah went against him. And Pharaoh Necho killed him at Megiddo when he confronted him.* [30] *Then his servants moved his body in a chariot from Megiddo, brought him to Jerusalem, and buried him in his own tomb. And the people of the land took Jehoahaz the son of Josiah, anointed him, and made him king in his father's place.*

9. **Second Chronicles 35:20-24**—*After all this, when Josiah had prepared the temple, Necho king of Egypt came up to fight against Carchemish by the Euphrates; and Josiah went out against him.* [21] *But* ***he sent messengers to him, saying, "What have I to do with you, king of Judah? I have not come against you this day, but against the house with which I have war; for God commanded me to make haste. Refrain from meddling with God, who is with me, lest He destroy you."*** [22] ***Nevertheless Josiah would not turn his face***

***from him**, but disguised himself so that he might fight with him, and did not heed the words of Necho from the mouth of God. So he came to fight in the Valley of Megiddo.* [23] *And the archers shot King Josiah; and the king said to his servants, "Take me away, for I am severely wounded."* [24] *His servants therefore took him out of that chariot and put him in the second chariot that he had, and they brought him to Jerusalem. So he died, and was buried in one of the tombs of his fathers. And all Judah and Jerusalem mourned for Josiah.*

10. **Isaiah 45:1-3 KJV**—*Thus saith the LORD to his anointed, to Cyrus, whose right hand I have holden, to subdue nations before him; and I will loose the loins of kings, to open before him the two leaved gates; and the gates shall not be shut;* [2] *I will go before thee, and make the crooked places straight: I will break in pieces the gates of brass, and cut in sunder the bars of iron:* [3] *And I will give thee the treasures of darkness, and hidden riches of secret places, that thou mayest know that I, the LORD, which call thee by thy name, am the God of Israel.*

11. **Isaiah 44:28**—*Who says of Cyrus, "He is My shepherd, and he shall perform all My pleasure, saying to Jerusalem, 'You shall be built,' and to the temple, 'Your foundation shall be laid.'"*

12. **Isaiah 45:1-13**—*Thus says the LORD to His anointed, to Cyrus, whose right hand I have held—to subdue nations before him and loose the armor of kings, to open before him the double doors, so that the gates will not be shut:* [2] *"I will go before you and make the crooked places straight; I will break in pieces the gates of bronze and cut the bars of iron.* [3] *I will give you the treasures of darkness and hidden riches of secret places, that you may know that I, the LORD, Who call you by your name, Am the God of Israel.* [4] *For Jacob My servant's sake, and Israel My elect, I have even called you by your name; I have named you, though you have not known Me.* [5] *I am the LORD, and there is no other; there is no God besides Me. I will gird you, though you have not known Me,* [6] *That they may know from the rising of the sun to its setting that there is none besides Me. I am the LORD, and there is no other;* [7] *I form the light and create darkness, I make peace and create calamity; I, the LORD, do all these things.'* [8] *Rain down, you heavens, from above, and let the skies pour down righteousness; let the earth open, let them bring forth salvation, and let righteousness spring up together. I, the LORD, have created it.* [9] *Woe to him who strives with his Maker! Let the potsherd strive with the potsherds of the earth! Shall the clay say to him who forms it, 'What are you making?' Or shall your handiwork say, 'He has no hands'?* [10] *Woe to him who says to his father, 'What are you begetting?' Or to the woman, 'What have you brought forth?'"* [11] *Thus says the LORD, the Holy One of Israel, and his Maker: "Ask Me of things to come concerning My sons; and*

concerning the work of My hands, you command Me. [12] I have made the earth, and created man on it. I—My hands—stretched out the heavens, and all their host I have commanded. [13] I have raised him up in righteousness, and I will direct all his ways; He shall build My city and let My exiles go free, not for price nor reward," says the L*ORD of hosts.*

13. **Second Chronicles 36:22-23**—*Now in the first year of Cyrus king of Persia, that the word of the* L*ORD by the mouth of Jeremiah might be fulfilled, the* L*ORD stirred up the spirit of Cyrus king of Persia, so that he made a proclamation throughout all his kingdom, and also put it in writing, saying, [23] Thus says Cyrus king of Persia: All the kingdoms of the earth the* L*ORD God of heaven has given me. And He has commanded me to build Him a house at Jerusalem which is in Judah. Who is among you of all His people? May the* L*ORD his God be with him, and let him go up!*

14. **Daniel 5:2-6**—*While he tasted the wine, Belshazzar gave the command to bring the gold and silver vessels which his father Nebuchadnezzar had taken from the temple which had been in Jerusalem, that the king and his lords, his wives, and his concubines might drink from them. [3] Then they brought the gold vessels that had been taken from the temple of the house of God which had been in Jerusalem; and the king and his lords, his wives, and his concubines drank from them. [4] They drank wine, and praised the gods of gold and silver, bronze and iron, wood and stone. [5] In the same hour the fingers of a man's hand appeared and wrote opposite the lampstand on the plaster of the wall of the king's palace; and the king saw the part of the hand that wrote. [6] Then the king's countenance changed, and his thoughts troubled him, so that the joints of his hips were loosened and his knees knocked against each other.*

15. **Daniel 5:24-29**—*Then the fingers of the hand were sent from Him, and this writing was written. [25] "And this is the inscription that was written: MENE, MENE, TEKEL, UPHARSIN. [26] This is the interpretation of each word. MENE: God has numbered your kingdom, and finished it; [27] TEKEL: You have been weighed in the balances, and found wanting; [28] PERES: Your kingdom has been divided, and given to the Medes and Persians." [29] Then Belshazzar gave the command, and they clothed Daniel with purple and put a chain of gold around his neck, and made a proclamation concerning him that he should be the third ruler in the kingdom.*

16. **Daniel 5:30-31**—*That very night Belshazzar, king of the Chaldeans, was slain. [31] And Darius the Mede received the kingdom, being about sixty-two years old.*

17. **Isaiah 44:27**—*Who says to the deep, "Be dry! And I will dry up your rivers."*

THE KING TORE HIS GARMENTS

In 2 Kings 22, we see how King Josiah heard the Book of the Law, was cut to the heart, and responded in anguish at the state of the people, which included wicked practices that went against everything he had heard. King Josiah's father, Amon, and his grandfather, Manasseh, both did evil in the sight of the Lord (*see* 2 Kings 21). This will explain how Josiah had no knowledge of the Law. Imagine the agony he felt knowing that all he had known and experienced went against the God of his people. Some of the evil things that took place during this time were idolatry, child sacrifice (Manasseh even sacrificed his own son to pagan worship), and the presence of pagan shrines in Jerusalem. It's understandable why Josiah was so upset to the point of tearing his clothes.

A GENERATION CUT TO THE HEART

King Josiah was prophesied about hundreds of years before he was born. God had a plan for him, and He has a plan for you. Esther 4:14 says, *"For if you remain completely silent at this time, relief and deliverance will arise for the Jews from another place, but you and your father's house will perish. Yet who knows whether you have come to the kingdom for such a time as this?"* Considering the phrase "for such a time as this," how does this idea help you know that God has a calling and a plan for you in this time and season?

____

____

____

____

____

____

____

PROPHESYING AGAINST AN EVIL OBJECT

FOCUS POINT

In 1 Kings 13:1-2, it says, *"And behold,* ***a man of God*** *went from Judah to Bethel by the word of the Lord, and Jeroboam stood by the altar to burn incense. Then he cried out against the altar by the word of the Lord, and said, 'O altar, altar! Thus says the Lord: "Behold, a child, Josiah by name, shall be born to the house of*

David; and on you he shall sacrifice the priests of the high places who burn incense on you, and men's bones shall be burned on you.'"""

God sent a man of God hundreds of years in advance to prophesy and intercede on behalf of Josiah. He also cried out against the evil he foresaw. This reveals the importance of intercession. Consider your own life. How many people before you could have prayed for and interceded on your behalf? We won't know the exact number, but it is something to consider. How does that make you feel? Take this time to intercede for your future generation. Be the man or woman of God who stands in that place to speak life over the future. Write your answers and prayers.

JOSIAH MISSED GOD AT THE END, A WARNING TO THOSE GOD RAISES

Second Kings 23:25 states that there was no king before or after Josiah like him, because none was found who had turned to God with all their heart, soul, and might according to the Law of Moses. Once Josiah learned the truth of the Law, he immediately went into action and changed his life, fulfilling the prophecy spoken about him. The devil observes those dedicated to the Lord and set apart with a God-mandated calling. How can believers remain faithful to the Lord so that they not only start well but also finish well?

JOSIAH ATTEMPTED TO INTERVENE ON THE ACTIONS OF PHARAOH NECO, WHO WAS APPOINTED BY GOD

Disobedience led Josiah to alter the prophetic word given to him. He had the chance to back away from Pharaoh Neco; however, he chose to disguise himself so he could go forth and disobey. As in the garden, where Eve and Adam sinned and hid, Josiah chose to hide himself. Why do you think disobedience and hiding go hand in hand?

____

____

____

____

____

____

CYRUS THE ANOINTED

God referred to Cyrus as His "anointed." This means that God chose Cyrus, a pagan king, to end the Babylonian exile, allowing the Jewish people to return to Jerusalem and rebuild the temple. This is an example of God using even the unsaved to fulfill prophecy, as seen in 2 Chronicles 36:22-23.

THE RELIGIONS OF CYRUS

Cyrus had his own religion; however, in Ezra 1:2, it says, *"Thus says Cyrus king of Persia: All the kingdoms of the earth the Lord God of heaven has given me. And He has commanded me to build Him a house at Jerusalem which is in Judah."* God revealed to Cyrus that he would take part in building His house. Why do you think God would use a pagan king to do this important task?

____

____

____

____

____

____

GOD USED CYRUS TO BREAK IN PIECES THE GATES OF BRONZE, AND TO CUT THE BARS OF IRON

When someone is anointed by God to do something, it doesn't matter if the situation is impossible; it will be done. The task is never too hard for God. He equips those He desires to use with the strength and ability to complete the job. The important point is that He needs willing vessels who will rise to the task.

THE KING OF BABYLON WAS REJECTED

Once again, we see the father's teachings passed down to the son. The disrespect shown toward the items taken from the temple proves that Belshazzar had no understanding of the God of Israel. Not only did he defile these items, but he did so in the presence of his lords, wives, and concubines. Why do you believe that someone would encourage those around to not only watch but also partake in sin?

____

____

____

____

____

____

THE WRITING WAS ON THE WALL!

Imagine a hand appearing and writing a mysterious message on the wall! This scene was so frightening that it affected the king's physical response. Because he lacked understanding of the One True God, he would not have experienced a supernatural event like this. What do you think the response of those with him would have been, given the king's reaction?

____

____

____

____

____

____

THE INSCRIPTION THAT WAS WRITTEN

Based on the interpretation of the writing, what do you think Belshazzar and those with him thought about those words, and that his life would be over soon?

THAT VERY NIGHT, BABYLON WAS CONQUERED, BUT NOT DESTROYED

That same night, Belshazzar was slain. The message written on the wall was fulfilled immediately after Daniel revealed its meaning to Belshazzar. In Daniel 5:29, the king put a purple robe on Daniel, gave him a gold chain for his neck, and made him the third ruler in the kingdom. Why do you think he did this instead of repenting?

GOD'S PERSONAL LETTER TO CYRUS

The idea that Cyrus might have heard about the prophecy concerning him is remarkable. Even the detail of how they dried the rivers to conquer Babylon. Read 1 Corinthians 14:24. Why do you think prophecy is vital for those who hear it?

CYRUS RESPONDED TO THE PROPHECY

PERSONAL REFLECTIONS

God used a pagan king to release the exiles and send them back to Judah to rebuild the temple of God. The term "Cyrus the Great" has come up recently. When God uses a man to help a nation, it echoes the calling of Cyrus. Given the current state of our culture, we need to pray that those in office are used by God, even if they are unsaved. We need to cover them with intercessory prayers and ask God to send workers, harvesters, to minister to them. Take this time to pray for the leaders of your nation. Ask God to place in office those who can be used by God. Write down your prayer and anything you hear the Lord speaking to you.

SECTION TWO

The Present Evil Age

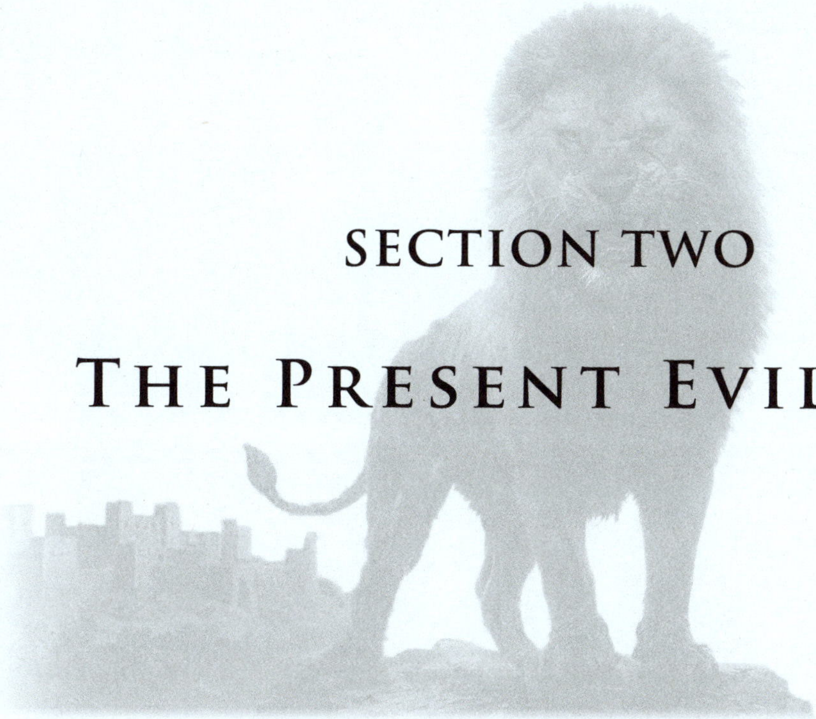

CHAPTER SEVEN

THE NEO-BABEL AGENDA

SCRIPTURES

1. **Luke 4:5-8**—*Then the devil, taking Him up on a high mountain, showed Him all the kingdoms of the world in a moment of time.*[6] *And the devil said to Him, "All this authority I will give You, and their glory; for this has been delivered to me, and I give it to whomever I wish.*[7] *Therefore, if You will worship before me, all will be Yours."*[8] *And Jesus answered and said to him, "Get behind Me, Satan! For it is written, 'You shall worship the* LORD *your God, and Him only you shall serve.'"*

2. **First Samuel 17**—*Due to the length of the text, please read from your Bible.*

3. **Luke 4:5 NIV**—*The devil led him up to a high place and showed him* ***in an instant*** *all the kingdoms of the world.*

4. **First Peter 5:8-9**—*Be sober, be vigilant; because your adversary the devil walks about like a roaring lion, seeking whom he may devour.*[9] *Resist him, steadfast in the faith, knowing that the same sufferings are experienced by your brotherhood in the world.*

5. **Proverbs 10:22**—*The blessing of the* LORD *makes one rich, and He adds no sorrow with it.*

6. **Psalm 75:4-7**—*I said to the boastful, "Do not deal boastfully," and to the wicked, "Do not lift up the horn.*[5] *Do not lift up your horn on high; do not speak with a stiff neck."*[6] *For exaltation comes neither from the east nor from the west nor from the south.*[7] *But God is the Judge: He puts down one, and exalts another.*

7. **Psalm 73:1-16**—*Truly God is good to Israel, to such as are pure in heart.* [2] *But as for me,* ***my feet had almost stumbled; my steps had nearly slipped. 3 For I was envious of the boastful, when I saw the prosperity of the wicked.*** [4] *For there are no pangs in their death, but their strength is firm.* [5] *They are not in trouble as other men, nor are they plagued like other men.* [6] *Therefore pride serves as their necklace; violence covers them like a garment.* [7] *Their eyes bulge with abundance; they have more than heart could wish.* [8] *They scoff and speak wickedly concerning oppression; they speak loftily.* [9] *They set their mouth against the heavens, and their tongue walks through the earth.* [10] *Therefore his people return here, and waters of a full cup are drained by them.* [11] *And they say, "How does God know? And is there knowledge in the Most High?"* [12] ***Behold, these are the ungodly, who are always at ease; they increase in riches. 13 Surely I have cleansed my heart in vain, and washed my hands in innocence.*** [14] *For all day long I have been plagued, and chastened every morning.* [15] *If I had said, "I will speak thus," Behold, I would have been untrue to the generation of Your children.* [16] ***When I thought how to understand this, it was too painful for me.***

8. **Psalm 73:17-20**—*Until I went into the sanctuary of God; then I understood their end.* [18] *Surely You set them in slippery places; You cast them down to destruction.* [19] ***Oh, how they are brought to desolation, as in a moment! They are utterly consumed with terrors.*** [20] *As a dream when one awakes, so, Lord, when You awake, You shall despise their image.*

9. **Second Corinthians 11:14**—*And no wonder! For Satan himself transforms himself into an angel of light.*

10. **Romans 1:21-25**—*Because, although they knew God, they did not glorify Him as God, nor were thankful, but became futile in their thoughts, and their foolish hearts were darkened.* [22] *Professing to be wise, they became fools,* [23] *and changed the glory of the incorruptible God into an image made like corruptible man—and birds and four-footed animals and creeping things.* [24] *Therefore God also gave them up to uncleanness, in the lusts of their hearts, to dishonor their bodies among themselves,* [25] *who exchanged the truth of God for the lie, and worshiped and served the creature rather than the Creator, who is blessed forever. Amen.*

11. **Matthew 6:22-23**—*The lamp of the body is the eye. If therefore your eye is good, your whole body will be full of light.* [23] *But if your eye is bad, your whole body will be full of darkness. If therefore the light that is in you is darkness, how great is that darkness!*

12. **Luke 11:34-36**—*The lamp of the body is the eye. Therefore, when your eye is good, your whole body also is full of light. But when your eye is bad, your body also is full of darkness.* [35] *Therefore take heed that the light which is in you is not darkness.* [36] *If then your whole*

body is full of light, having no part dark, the whole body will be full of light, as when the bright shining of a lamp gives you light.

13. **Luke 11:16**— *Others, testing Him, sought from Him a sign from heaven.*

14. **Luke 11:29**—*And while the crowds were thickly gathered together, He began to say, "This is an evil generation. It seeks a sign, and no sign will be given to it except the sign of Jonah the prophet."*

15. **Luke 8:16**—*No one, when he has lit a lamp, covers it with a vessel or puts it under a bed, but sets it on a lampstand, that those who enter may see the light.*

16. **Luke 11:33**—*No one, when he has lit a lamp, puts it in a secret place or under a basket, but on a lampstand, that those who come in may see the light.*

17. **Proverbs 20:27**—*The spirit of a man is the lamp of the* Lord, *searching all the inner depths of his heart.*

18. **Ephesians 1:17-18**—*That the God of our Lord Jesus Christ, the Father of glory, may give to you the spirit of wisdom and revelation in the knowledge of Him,* [18] *the eyes of your understanding being enlightened; that you may know what is the hope of His calling, what are the riches of the glory of His inheritance in the saints.*

19. **Ephesians 5:14**—*Therefore He says: "Awake, you who sleep, arise from the dead, and Christ will give you light."*

20. **Proverbs 4:18 NASB1995**—*But the path of the righteous is like the light of dawn, that shines brighter and brighter until the full day.*

21. **First John 1:5**—*This is the message which we have heard from Him and declare to you, that God is light and in Him is no darkness at all.*

22. **Genesis 11**—*Due to the length of the text, please read from your Bible.*

23. **Revelation 9:1-11**—*Then the fifth angel sounded: And I saw a star fallen from heaven to the earth. To him was given the key to the bottomless pit.* [2] *And he opened the bottomless pit, and smoke arose out of the pit like the smoke of a great furnace. So the sun and the air were darkened because of the smoke of the pit.* [3] *Then out of the smoke locusts came upon the earth. And to them was given power, as the scorpions of the earth have power.* [4] *They were commanded not to harm the grass of the earth, or any green thing, or any tree,*

but only those men who do not have the seal of God on their foreheads. [5] *And they were not given authority to kill them, but to torment them for five months. Their torment was like the torment of a scorpion when it strikes a man.* [6] *In those days men will seek death and will not find it; they will desire to die, and death will flee from them.* [7] *The shape of the locusts was like horses prepared for battle. On their heads were crowns of something like gold, and their faces were like the faces of men.* [8] *They had hair like women's hair, and their teeth were like lions' teeth.* [9] *And they had breastplates like breastplates of iron, and the sound of their wings was like the sound of chariots with many horses running into battle.* [10] *They had tails like scorpions, and there were stings in their tails. Their power was to hurt men five months.* [11] *And they had as king over them the angel of the bottomless pit, whose name in Hebrew is Abaddon, but in Greek he has the name Apollyon.*

24. **Revelation 20**—*Due to the length of the text, please read from your Bible.*

Satan is a master deceiver who has convinced many throughout the generations to believe his lies and to be used for his Luciferian agenda. Read John 8:44, 1 John 3:8, and Revelation 12:9, and write down the common descriptions of the devil.

____

____

____

____

____

____

____

THE HIGH PLACE OF CONTRACTUAL AGREEMENT WITH SATAN

The desire for "more" has been around since the beginning. In today's culture, people are dissatisfied with what they have. It's not enough. The need for more money, more things, more of this and that. More, more, more. Because of this, it must be easy for the devil to come and offer these people more than they want or ask for. In what ways should the believer avoid these offers from the enemy?

____

____

THE DEVIL SEEKS WHOM HE MAY DEVOUR

The devil is full of hate. If he weren't, he wouldn't want to devour people. The fact that he isn't devouring everyone on the planet means he's not allowed to. As stated in the main book, he doesn't have the authority to do so. Cooperation is the key. In what ways do people cooperate with the devil and allow him to "devour" them?

DARKNESS SETS OUT TO DISCOURAGE BELIEVERS BY PARADING THE SUCCESS OF THE WICKED

When people pursue the riches of this world, fame, and abundance of possessions, they believe that having it all will bring them great joy. This is another lie the enemy tells. He portrays this "wealth" as the only thing someone needs. The truth is that many who have this form of wealth, fame, and success are still unhappy and dissatisfied. Do you believe this to be true? If so, why?

GODLY PROMOTION IS THE HIGHEST PROMOTION AND IS A CLEAN INCREASE

As previously stated, those who pursue riches often experience sorrow. The opposite is true of God. He adds no sorrow. Praise God. He wants to bless His people without strings attached. John 10:10 says that God gives abundant life. Abundant life is everything needed in this life, but in abundance. God knows the need before it's even spoken, and He wants to give abundantly. Thank God for the blessing.

HOW THE BELIEVER SHOULD RESPOND TO THE SUCCESS OF WICKEDNESS

Given the fate of the wicked, even when it seems they are receiving more and aren't facing consequences this side of eternity, how should the believer respond to the success they observe among the wicked?

A HORRIFYING END TO THE WICKED—TERROR AND DOOM

FOCUS POINT

Second Peter 3:9 ends with God's statement that He is *"not willing that any should perish but that all should come to repentance."* In His patience and kindness, God gives everyone a chance to turn to Him. Why? Because He knows the fate of the wicked and doesn't want anyone to experience it. However, people have free will and can choose whom to serve. Sadly, many will choose the wide and broad way. Matthew 7:13-14 says, *"Enter by the narrow gate; for wide is the gate and broad is the way that leads to destruction, and there are many who go in by it.* [14] *Because narrow is the gate and difficult is the way which leads to life, and there are few who find it."* Read Romans 1. What does God do when people choose ungodly, vile, and evil acts instead of God? How does this passage reveal the outcome of these actions?

____

____

____

____

____

____

____

LUCIFERIAN PATTERN OF DEFIANCE AND THEIR COSMIC STUNTS

Lucifer is often portrayed as a bringer of knowledge, enlightenment, and self-empowerment. As believers, we know this to be false. He is the father of lies, the master deceiver, jealous of God and everything He can do. Because of this, he is a copycat, perverts all things good, and masquerades as an angel of light. The word "masquerade" means *to disguise oneself, to assume the appearance of something one is not.*[1] The only way Satan can truly deceive people is by disguising himself as something he is not. To the Luciferians, he portrays himself as light and as God.

THE REMOVAL OF GOD FROM THEIR THINKING OPENS THE DOOR TO LUCIFERIAN IDEOLOGY

We know why Satan wants people to turn from God, but why do you think people reach a point where they would rather believe a lie, such as that there is no God or that the devil is a god?

____

____

GENEROUS OR STINGY, A SIGN OF A GOOD EYE OR A BAD EYE

A generous person has a good eye, whereas a stingy person has a bad one. With this in mind, how do Matthew 6:22-23 and Luke 11:34-36 apply to the Luciferian agenda?

JESUS IS THE LIGHT

John 8:12 says, *"Then Jesus spoke to them again, saying, 'I am the light of the world. He who follows Me shall not walk in darkness, but have the light of life.'"* When we are focused on Jesus, the true light, we will not walk in darkness. We will be able to identify all things that are not of God, and it will be evident in our lives to those around us. Read 1 John 1:7. What takes place when a believer walks in the light?

REVELATION KNOWLEDGE

When a person receives the revelation of Jesus, it brings understanding of His calling, the hope He offers, and the glorious riches of His inheritance. God gives the spirit of wisdom and revelation, which are needed to fully discover all that Jesus has provided. Take this time to thank God for revealing these things to you.

LIGHT LEADS TO AN ILLUMINATED LIFE AND JOURNEY

The righteous will shine ever more brightly over time, illuminating the surrounding darkness. What will this look like, and how will the world recognize this light?

____

____

____

____

____

____

LUCIFERIAN LIGHT IS FALSE KNOWLEDGE

It's an interesting fact that Luciferians worship light, even though Jesus is the true light. Instead, they worship a lie rather than reality. They will come to their senses when the devil is revealed for who he is. Unfortunately, by then it will be too late to change their minds.

PORTALS ARE BEING OPENED

Those who follow Satan and believe his lies are in for a rude awakening. They are messing with things they don't fully understand and the repercussions of their actions. What do you think will be going through these people's minds when they experience the Revelation 9 scenario?

____

____

____

____

THE CRUCIAL PIECE

PERSONAL REFLECTIONS

The Church, the *Ekklesia,* is the crucial piece of what's going on in the world today. Without the Church, evil would prevail. You are here for this time for a reason. To stand in the gap and intercede for a lost and dying world—a world on its way to an eternity of separation from God and eternal punishment. It's amazing how those who follow Lucifer are devoted enough to cause havoc in the spiritual realm against believers. Let's take a stand and be even more devoted to Jesus, a light to those around us. What each individual needs is an encounter with the One True Living God, which they can experience by seeing an obedient believer in Jesus being a light to a lost and dying world. Take this time to pray for those you personally know who need Jesus. Write down their names and what you hear the Holy Spirit saying to you.

CHAPTER EIGHT

KINGDOMS COLLIDE IN TERRITORIAL WARFARE

SCRIPTURES

1. **Matthew 28:18-20**—*And Jesus came and spoke to them, saying, "All authority has been given to Me in heaven and on earth.* [19] *Go therefore and make disciples of all the nations, baptizing them in the name of the Father and of the Son and of the Holy Spirit,* [20] *teaching them to observe all things that I have commanded you; and lo, I am with you always, even to the end of the age." Amen.*

2. **First John 3:2**—*Beloved, now we are children of God; and it has not yet been revealed what we shall be, but we know that when He is revealed, **we shall be like Him, for we shall see Him as He is.***

3. **Hebrews 13:8**—*Jesus Christ is the same yesterday, today, and forever.*

4. **Proverbs 29:2**—*When the righteous are in authority, the people rejoice; but when a wicked man rules, the people groan.*

5. **First John 5:4**—*For whatever is born of God overcomes the world. And this is the victory that has overcome the world—our faith.*

6. **First John 4:4**—*You are of God, little children, and have overcome them, **because He who is in you is greater than he who is in the world**.*

7. **Revelation 12:11**—*And they overcame him by the blood of the Lamb and by the word of their testimony, and they did not love their lives to the death.*

8. **First John 4:17**—*Love has been perfected among us in this: that we may have boldness in the day of judgment; because as He is, so are we in this world.*

9. **Galatians 1:4**—*Who gave Himself for our sins, that He might deliver us from this present evil age, according to the will of our God and Father.*

10. **Luke 1:17**—*He will also go before Him in the spirit and power of Elijah, "to turn the hearts of the fathers to the children," and the disobedient to the wisdom of the just, to make ready a people prepared for the Lord.*

11. **Romans 8:14**—*For as many as are led by the Spirit of God, these are sons of God.*

Before Jesus, there was no church body. The terms "brother" and "sister in Christ" didn't exist. The distinction between those who knew the God of the Old Testament and those who didn't was Jewish and Gentile. Today, we are the Church, and anyone who accepts Jesus as their Lord and Savior can join the family. Thank God for Jesus, who made a way for all to have access to Him, and for the Holy Spirit.

JESUS IS THE SAME YESTERDAY, TODAY, AND FOREVER!

Given that Jesus is the same yesterday, today, and forever, how does this truth shape your perspective on God's promises for the future?

____

____

____

____

____

____

WHERE DOES EXPLORATION IN THE HEART OF MAN ORIGINATE?

The longing to explore—whether venturing into space, descending into the depths of the oceans, or uncovering the mysteries of ancient civilizations—seems built into humanity's very being. If the desire to explore is rooted in God's original mandate to Adam, how might our curiosity and drive for discovery be fulfilled in the age to come?

EXPLORATION IS A KINGDOM PIECE DORMANT WITHIN HUMANITY, EXPRESSED THROUGH THE NEED TO DISCOVER

The idea that God's people could expand His kingdom to the farthest corners of the universe is quite spectacular. Today, we have a very limited ability to reach into space. There are many complications and risks involved in venturing into the universe. What are your thoughts on whether we could possibly expand the kingdom of God into places we could never imagine?

THIS CURRENT TERRITORY WAY

FOCUS POINT

When someone knows their territory is under threat of attack, the natural response is to prepare. Prepare for battle, and winning is the only option. Having weapons ready, in the proper position, wearing protective gear, and having ammunition is vital for territorial war. Winning will never come from being lazy, sitting back, or ignoring threats. Be proactive, sharp, and ready in and out of season, knowing that the battle can start at any moment. This is a real-life scenario; however, in the spiritual sense, many people don't take the territorial war between God and the devil over the individual as seriously. In what ways can a believer be ready for this type of territorial war? What steps are you taking so that you win every time?

THE GREAT COMMISSION

Once a person wins their territorial war, the next battle is with the next person. How do victorious believers help equip those around them to become victorious as well? How does this idea relate to the Great Commission?

CONQUERING POWER THAT BRINGS THE WORLD TO ITS KNEES!

When the world sees believers overcome everything the enemy throws at them, it has no choice but to go to its knees. When a believer overcomes, it builds faith, an active, world-changing force capable of pushing back darkness and making a tangible impact in their generation.

AS HE IS, SO ARE WE IN THIS WORLD!

We are in the last days; it is not the time for believers to cower and let the Luciferian system take over. How does a person walk in boldness until the day of judgment?

GOD'S WILL FOR YOU IS TO BE DELIVERED FROM THIS PRESENT EVIL AGE!

God desires to deliver us from this present evil age. What do you think this looks like?

REFORMATION

Turning the hearts of fathers to the children is needed today. In today's culture, we see that fathers, both spiritual and natural, are absent from their children. The result is rebellion, a lack of guidance, vulnerability, and hostility. Reformation is needed to "reform" what has been broken. When fathers rise to their God-given assignment, revival can come. Do you believe this to be true? Why or why not?

THE KINGDOM OF JESUS IS COMING

PERSONAL REFLECTIONS

Second Corinthians 3:18 says, *"But we all, with unveiled face, beholding as in a mirror the glory of the Lord, are being transformed into the same image from* ***glory to glory,*** *just as by the Spirit of the Lord."* Going from glory to glory means moving from the Old Testament Covenant to the New Testament Covenant. The Law was given in the Old Covenant, and Jesus was given for the New Covenant. Because of this, believers are set free from a works-based gospel to the gospel of grace, forgiveness, and freedom. Believers are equipped to get through even the darkest days ahead. Remember, spiritual victory is not about avoiding hardship but about standing firm and trusting God, even when circumstances are difficult. With this in mind, how can you identify your role within the body of Christ to help you align with the Great Commission?

CHAPTER NINE

A Blood-Bought Believer Carries Force for Cultural Impact!

SCRIPTURES

1. **Matthew 16:18**—*...and on this rock I will build My church, and the gates of Hades shall not prevail against it.*

2. **John 3:5**—*Jesus answered, "Most assuredly, I say to you,* ***unless one is born of water and the Spirit, he cannot enter the kingdom of God****."*

3. **Genesis 3:15 NIV**—*And I will put enmity between you and the woman, and between your offspring and hers; he will crush your head, and you will strike his heel.*

4. **John 1:14**—*And the Word became flesh and dwelt among us, and we beheld His glory, the glory as of the only begotten of the Father, full of grace and truth.*

5. **First John 4:4**—*You are of God, little children, and have overcome them, because He who is in you is greater than he who is in the world.*

6. **Hebrews 6:9-12**—*But, beloved, we are confident of better things concerning you, yes,
things that accompany salvation, though we speak in this manner. [10] For God is not unjust to
forget your work and labor of love which you have shown toward His name, in that you have
ministered to the saints, and do minister. [11] And we desire that each one of you show the same
diligence to the full assurance of hope until the end, [12] that you do not become sluggish, but
imitate those who through faith and patience inherit the promises.*

7. **Luke 17:21**—*Nor will they say, "See here!" or "See there!" For indeed, the kingdom of God is within you.*

8. **Romans 14:17**—*For the kingdom of God is not eating and drinking, but righteousness and peace and joy in the Holy Spirit.*

9. **Revelation 12:11**—*And they overcame him by the blood of the Lamb and by the word of their testimony, and they did not love their lives to the death.*

10. **Galatians 1:12**—*For I neither received it from man, nor was I taught it, but it came through the revelation of Jesus Christ.*

11. **Galatians 2:20**—*I have been crucified with Christ; it is no longer I who live, but Christ lives in me; and the life which I now live in the flesh* ***I live by faith in the Son of God****, who loved me and gave Himself for me.*

12. **First Corinthians 6:17**—*But he who is joined to the Lord is* ***one spirit with Him.***

13. **Second Corinthians 5:17**—*Therefore, if anyone is in Christ, he is a new creation; old things have passed away; behold, all things have become new.*

14. **Second Corinthians 5:17 AMPC**—*Therefore if any person is [ingrafted] in Christ (the Messiah) he is a new creation (a new creature altogether); the old [previous moral and spiritual condition] has passed away. Behold, the fresh and new has come!*

15. **Hebrews 12:23**—*To the general assembly and church of the firstborn who are registered in heaven, to God the Judge of all, to* ***the spirits of just men made perfect.***

16. **Romans 8:29**—*For whom He foreknew, He also predestined to be conformed to the image of His Son, that* ***He might be the firstborn among many brethren.***

17. **First John 4:17**—*Love has been perfected among us in this: that we may have boldness in the day of judgment; because as He is, so are we in this world.*

18. **Galatians 1:6-9**—*I marvel that you are turning away so soon from Him who called you in the grace of Christ, to a different gospel,* [7] *which is not another; but there are some who trouble you and want to pervert the gospel of Christ.* [8] *But even if we, or an angel from heaven, preach any other gospel to you than what we have preached to you, let him be accursed.* [9] *As we have said before, so now I say again, if anyone preaches any other gospel to you than what you have received, let him be accursed.*

19. **Galatians 3:1-5, 10-12**—*O foolish Galatians! Who has bewitched you that you should not obey the truth, before whose eyes Jesus Christ was clearly portrayed among you as crucified? [2] This only I want to learn from you: Did you receive the Spirit by the works of the law, or by the hearing of faith? [3] Are you so foolish? Having begun in the Spirit, are you now being made perfect by the flesh? [4] Have you suffered so many things in vain—if indeed it was in vain? [5] Therefore He who supplies the Spirit to you and works miracles among you, does He do it by the works of the law, or by the hearing of faith? … [10] For as many as are of the works of the law are under the curse; for it is written, "Cursed is everyone who does not continue in all things which are written in the book of the law, to do them." [11] But that no one is justified by the law in the sight of God is evident, for "the just shall live by faith." [12] Yet the law is not of faith, but "the man who does them shall live by them."*

20. **Galatians 4:21–Galatians 5:4**—*Due to the length of the text, please read from your Bible.*

21. **Deuteronomy 27–28**—*Due to the length of the text, please read from your Bible.*

22. **Deuteronomy 13:1-18**—*Due to the length of the text, please read from your Bible.*

Many believers are walking around with no clue about the authority they have. They think that once they get saved, they receive only fire insurance. In what ways is this evident in the Christian culture today?

____

____

____

____

____

____

VESSELS OR PHYSICAL BODIES CARRY CARGO

Each person was created to be a carrier of something. This is either the Holy Spirit or the dark forces of the devil. What are the fruits of being filled with the Holy Spirit? What are the fruits of being filled with dark forces?

____

____

GOD OPERATES BY THE LAWS HE SET IN MOTION

At the moment Adam and Eve sinned, a redemption plan was set in place—Jesus! How did His victory over death, hell, and the grave change humanity's situation?

WHY DID IT TAKE 4,000 YEARS FOR JESUS TO ARRIVE?

Because Adam and Eve used their free will and accepted the serpent's words as truth, God needed willing people to speak forth His plan. Thankfully, throughout history, people have chosen God and let Him use their voices to speak these things and prepare the way prophetically for the arrival of Jesus and His redemption.

THE PROPHESIED WORD BECAME FLESH 4,000 YEARS AFTER THE FALL OF ADAM

Some say Jesus fulfilled between 300 and 600 prophecies! Isn't that incredible? The likelihood of a single prophecy coming true is remarkable, let alone hundreds. Considering this, how do these figures influence your view of prophecy?

UNTIL JESUS, ALL WERE TRAPPED UNDER THE DOMINION OF DARKNESS

FOCUS POINT

Imagine a world where the devil could rule, reign, and possess people, and there was nothing anyone could do about it. For believers, this is hard to understand because we do have authority over the enemy. The situation is different for unbelievers. They don't know about the freedom offered by Jesus, let alone that they could overcome the enemy if they turned to Him. Now, imagine how the devil and his minions felt the moment Jesus was born! In the New Testament, there are several examples of demons freaking out when Jesus appeared where they were. Read Matthew 8:28-34. What was the demons' response to seeing Jesus? Why do you think they were afraid of Him?

WE CAN BE CONFIDENT OF BETTER THINGS IN THE NEW COVENANT!

How does the assurance in Hebrews 6:10, when it says that *"God is not unjust to forget your work and labor of love,"* encourage believers to remain diligent and steadfast in their faith, especially in challenging times?

THE PRESENCE OF MATURE BELIEVERS SHOULD DEMAND AN EXPLANATION!

Believers' lives should demand an explanation because they display a fearless faith and authority that are not swayed by the chaos or hostility of the surrounding culture. This is not a passive faith. Instead, it is active, enduring, and even willing to face death. God will never overlook this faithfulness. He remembers it all!

THINGS THAT ACCOMPANY SALVATION

As previously stated, many believers are unaware of what they have when they are saved. This is exactly where the devil wants believers to remain. One of the devil's greatest fears is a believer who knows who they are in Christ and understands what they have through Him to overcome everything the devil throws their way. How has this understanding impacted you?

SEVEN PARTS TO YOUR SALVATION

Of the seven parts of salvation, is there anything on the list that you were not aware was given to you when you became born again? If so, write your answer.

A REVELATION OF JESUS IS CRUCIAL TO OVERCOME DARKNESS IN THIS WORLD

Receiving a revelation of Jesus and all He has provided through salvation is vital for all believers. Jesus wants to make Himself known. He desires to be sought after. Through this, He will reveal the truth of who He is to those who seek Him. Read Jeremiah 29:11-14. What does God say will happen when someone seeks Him with their whole heart?

RESIST WHAT DOES NOT ALIGN WITH WHAT JESUS PAID FOR

Martyrs who faced death with joy and confidence exemplify strength not in themselves but in their knowledge of what they possessed in Christ. They moved beyond a religious, performance-based mindset to one of faith empowered by grace and revelation.

RELIGION PREACHES DOING AND TRYING— IN JESUS, EVERYTHING IS DONE, AND THE BELIEVER IS NOW TRUSTING

What does it mean to you to be "a new creation in Christ," and how does that understanding shape your approach to living in the present age?

JESUS IS THE PROTOTYPE

Jesus set the example of how we should live. Throughout the New Testament, He has given us the tools and understanding, and He has even taught us how to pray. If you are at a loss for what to do, look through the Word to see how Jesus handled each situation. Take what you read and apply it to your life, and you can become just as victorious as He is!

THE DEVIL CAN'T BEAT THE CHURCH, SO HE ATTEMPTS TO JOIN IT!

Many in the Church are experiencing an identity crisis. This is due to a lack of knowledge of the Word and of who Jesus is. In what ways do you see this among believers?

THE DEVIL SOWS MESSAGES AND RELIGIOUS IDEOLOGIES CONTRARY TO THE TRUTH OF THE GOSPEL

There is danger when someone shifts their focus from the grace found in Jesus to a performance-based approach to faith. Legalism can creep into someone's heart and beliefs, undermining the core of the gospel. Faith based on what someone does for God, rather than on what Jesus has done for us, leads to spiritual bondage that robs this believer of the freedom and assurance that come from grace.

This is powerful, and we should understand that we cannot add anything to the finished work of the cross. It is only what Jesus did that matters. The good we do is a by-product of what He already did and paid for.

YOU ARE ANOINTED TO BE THE BEST THERE IS!

PERSONAL REFLECTIONS

Jesus paid it all. Salvation offers everything we need not only to survive but also to thrive in a culture going mad. In this chapter, it was revealed what is inherited at salvation by using the words *sozo* and *soteria*. Looking at the following list, after each word, write what you believe that means to you. Once you have done that, spend time with the Lord, thanking Him for everything He has provided for you and for revealing it to you in a new way.

Saved:

____

____

____

____

____

Delivered:

____

____

____

____

____

To Do Well. To Be Prosperous:

____

____

____

____

____

Preserved:

Protected:

Healed:

Made Whole:

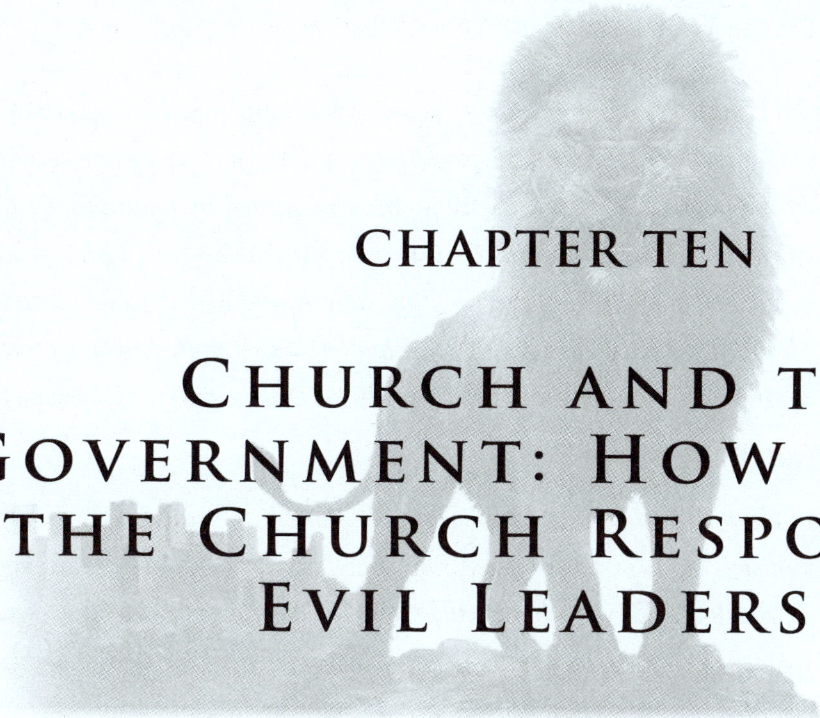

CHAPTER TEN

Church and the Government: How Should the Church Respond to Evil Leaders?

SCRIPTURES

1. **John 6:15**—*Therefore when Jesus perceived that they were about to come* ***and take Him by force to make Him king,*** *He departed again to the mountain by Himself alone.*

2. **Luke 6:15**—*Matthew and Thomas; James the son of Alphaeus, and* ***Simon called the Zealot.***

3. **Romans 13:1-4**—*Let every soul be subject to the governing authorities. For there is no authority except from God, and the authorities that exist are appointed by God. 2 Therefore whoever resists the authority resists the ordinance of God, and those who resist will bring judgment on themselves. 3 For* ***rulers are not a terror to good works, but to evil.*** *Do you want to be unafraid of the authority? Do what is good, and you will have praise from the same. 4 For* ***he is God's minister to you for good.*** *But if you do evil, be afraid; for he does not bear the sword in vain; for* ***he is God's minister, an avenger to execute wrath on him who practices evil.***

4. **Matthew 14:1-12**—*At that time Herod the tetrarch heard the report about Jesus 2 and said to his servants, "This is John the Baptist; he is risen from the dead, and therefore these powers are at work in him." 3 For Herod had laid hold of John and bound him, and put him in prison for the sake of Herodias, his brother Philip's wife. 4 Because John had said to him, "It is not lawful for you to have her." 5 And although he wanted to put him to death, he feared the*

multitude, because they counted him as a prophet. [6] *But when Herod's birthday was celebrated, the daughter of Herodias danced before them and pleased Herod.* [7] *Therefore he promised with an oath to give her whatever she might ask.* [8] *So she, having been prompted by her mother, said, "Give me John the Baptist's head here on a platter."* [9] *And the king was sorry; nevertheless, because of the oaths and because of those who sat with him, he commanded it to be given to her.* [10] *So he sent and had John beheaded in prison.* [11] *And his head was brought on a platter and given to the girl, and she brought it to her mother.* [12] *Then his disciples came and took away the body and buried it, and went and told Jesus.*

5. **Mark 6:14-29**—*Now King Herod heard of Him, for His name had become well known. And he said, "John the Baptist is risen from the dead, and therefore these powers are at work in him."* [15] *Others said, "It is Elijah." And others said, "It is the Prophet, or like one of the prophets."* [16] *But when Herod heard, he said, "This is John, whom I beheaded; he has been raised from the dead!"* [17] *For Herod himself had sent and laid hold of John, and bound him in prison for the sake of Herodias, his brother Philip's wife; for he had married her.* [18] *Because John had said to Herod, "It is not lawful for you to have your brother's wife."* [19] *Therefore Herodias held it against him and wanted to kill him, but she could not;* [20] *for Herod feared John, knowing that he was a just and holy man, and he protected him. And when he heard him, he did many things, and heard him gladly.* [21] *Then an opportune day came when Herod on his birthday gave a feast for his nobles, the high officers, and the chief men of Galilee.* [22] *And when Herodias' daughter herself came in and danced, and pleased Herod and those who sat with him, the king said to the girl, "Ask me whatever you want, and I will give it to you."* [23] *He also swore to her, "Whatever you ask me, I will give you, up to half my kingdom."* [24] *So she went out and said to her mother, "What shall I ask?" And she said, "The head of John the Baptist!"* [25] *Immediately she came in with haste to the king and asked, saying, "I want you to give me at once the head of John the Baptist on a platter."* [26] *And the king was exceedingly sorry; yet, because of the oaths and because of those who sat with him, he did not want to refuse her.* [27] *Immediately the king sent an executioner and commanded his head to be brought. And he went and beheaded him in prison,* [28] *brought his head on a platter, and gave it to the girl; and the girl gave it to her mother.* [29] *When his disciples heard of it, they came and took away his corpse and laid it in a tomb.*

6. **Luke 13:31-32**—*On that very day some Pharisees came, saying to Him, "Get out and depart from here, for Herod wants to kill You."* [32] *And He said to them, "**Go, tell that fox,** 'Behold, I cast out demons and perform cures today and tomorrow, and the third day I shall be perfected.'"*

7. **Revelation 17:1**—*Then one of the seven angels who had the seven bowls came and talked with me, saying to me, **"Come, I will show you the judgment of the great harlot who sits on many waters."***

8. **Revelation 17:6**—*I saw the woman,* ***drunk with the blood of the saints and with the blood of the martyrs of Jesus****. And when I saw her, I marveled with great amazement.*

9. **Psalm 65:7**—*You who still the noise of the seas, the noise of their waves, and the tumult of the peoples.*

10. **Isaiah 17:12-13**—*Woe to the multitude of many people who make a noise like the roar of the seas, and to the rushing of nations that make a rushing like the rushing of mighty waters! [13] The nations will rush like the rushing of many waters; but God will rebuke them and they will flee far away, and be chased like the chaff of the mountains before the wind, like a rolling thing before the whirlwind.*

11. **Revelation 1:10**—*I was in the Spirit on* ***the Lord's Day****, and I heard behind me a loud voice, as of a trumpet.*

12. **Isaiah 10:27 NASB1995**—*So it will be in that day, that his burden will be removed from* ***your shoulders*** *and his yoke* ***from your neck****, and the* ***yoke will be broken*** *because of fatness.*

THE FIRST-CENTURY ZEALOTS AND A WARNING

Throughout history, we see "zealot-like" groups rise against the governmental power of their time. These groups stand for a religious or political cause. Oftentimes, their approach is intense toward those who oppose their stance. Currently, have you seen this type of behavior in the culture? In what ways would you say they symbolize the zealots in the Bible?

____

____

____

____

____

____

JESUS WAS ALMOST FORCIBLY TAKEN AND SET AS KING

Jesus had a choice to become king while on earth. If He had agreed to it, He would have changed the entire narrative established from the very beginning. We know that Jesus is King and will reign on earth after the Tribulation. It would have been the wrong time for Him to become king then. Similarly, there are times when we are faced with something we know is ours, but the timing is off. Being in tune with the Holy Spirit is vital so we don't change the narrative of the long-term blessing. Let's be led by the Voice of God and follow Jesus' example.

SIMON THE ZEALOT WAS A DISCIPLE

FOCUS POINT

Simon the Zealot could have been one of the radicals who attended riots, opposed the government at the time, and prepared for the coming Messiah who would overthrow it. This changed in his life when He met Jesus. Many people are in a similar situation. Young and old are following something they believe to be true; what they need is an encounter with Jesus. All it takes is one word from the Lord, and lives can instantly be changed. Take this time to pray for those in the same position. Ask the Lord to send workers to the harvest. Seek the Holy Spirit and write down your prayer.

____

____

____

____

____

____

JESUS DEPARTED FROM THE PRESS OF THE PEOPLE WHO WOULD MAKE HIM KING PREMATURELY

What are your thoughts on the following statement: "Let it be known that the Church should be deeply involved in the political world and do everything in its power to bring righteousness to the land"?

____

____

____

PACIFISTS, THE EXTREME OPPOSITE OF ZEALOTS

Sadly, many in the Church believe the Church should not take part in politics. As a result, many will not vote. Instead, they will stay home and yet voice their opinion about the person in office. This is the opposite of what should take place. Believers should rise and be part of those who are appointed to high office. If the *Ekklesia* took this seriously, could it be that we would avoid many evil and corrupt leaders? It's a compelling thought.

SAINT TELEMACHUS THE HERMIT MONK STOPPED THE GLADIATOR GAMES IN ROME

It took over 650 years of gladiator games before someone stood up against them. Imagine a world where these were celebrated. The crowds cheered as men and women were torn apart and massacred. It's hard to believe people could be so cruel as to let this go on for so long. Thank God for people like Saint Telemachus, who take a stand against evil, even at the cost of their own lives. Can you think of anyone in our culture who has taken a costly stand against the evils of our time? Write about it.

SUBMISSION TO THE GOVERNMENT: THE ROMANS 13 QUESTION

Many have used Romans 13:1-4 to justify submitting to corrupt governments. Where do you stand on this passage of scripture and on governmental authorities?

ROMANS 13 WAS WRITTEN UNDER A MONARCHY

In Matthew 14:1-12 and Mark 6:14-29, John the Baptist confronted Herod's sinful behavior. He is another example of someone who spoke out against the evil of his time, even if it cost him his life. Matthew 14:9 says that Herod *was sorry*. He felt this way for several possible reasons. Herod respected and feared John and was reluctant to kill him because people perceived him as a prophet. Killing John could lead to revolt and unrest. This shows that even though John was beheaded, Herod knew the impact of this act could be dramatic.

JESUS CALLED HEROD A FOX

Jesus was not afraid to call Herod a fox. He did so after John was beheaded. It could be said that He knew why John was killed, yet that didn't stop Him from speaking about the political figures Herod and Herodias. Typically, people would cower and not speak so directly against someone after a scenario like John's, especially since they were the rulers in that area. That didn't stop Jesus. What are your thoughts on why Jesus had no fear in making this comment?

DO NOT RESIST THE ORDINANCE OF GOD

Romans 13:3 makes an important point for believers about those in authority. Rulers or those in authority are not supposed to bring terror or hardship upon people. With this in mind, how should a leader bring terror to the works of evil?

WHAT HAPPENS WHEN A RULER WHO IS APPOINTED FOR GOOD USES THEIR POSITION FOR EVIL?

Pharaoh is an example of a corrupt ruler who abused his position and brought hardship upon the people. Exodus 1:8-11 says, *"Now there arose a new king over Egypt, who did not know Joseph.* [9] *And he said to his people, 'Look, the people of the children of Israel are more and mightier than we;* [10] *come, let us **deal shrewdly with them,** lest they multiply, and it happen, in the event of war, that they also join our enemies and fight against us, and so go up out of the land.'* [11] *Therefore they set taskmasters over them to **afflict them with their burdens.**"* In this setting, Pharaoh was intimidated by the number of Israelites and the possibility that they might be mightier than he and his army. Because of this fear, he turned against the people and afflicted them.

Continuing in verse 12, *"But the more they afflicted them, the more they multiplied and grew. And they were in dread of the children of Israel."* Even amid intense hardship, the children of Israel continued to multiply and increase in number. Let this encourage you that even when the enemy or a wicked leader brings difficulties, you are not alone. The Word of God continues to spread swiftly, and the body of Christ is growing worldwide, which scares the enemy. The *Ekklesia* is a force the devil cannot overcome, and he knows it.

IN THE UNITED STATES OF AMERICA, THE MONARCHY IS *WE THE PEOPLE*

In the United States, *We the People* have the right to ensure that the leaders of the land uphold the truths of the Constitution and the Declaration of Independence. In what ways are we to do this?

A BIBLICAL FIDUCIARY'S RESPONSIBILITY

The Pledge of Allegiance is a symbol of patriotism and loyalty to the United States of America. It was written to encourage school-aged children to understand the importance of the nation being under God and of walking in liberty and justice for all.

EACH NATION IS DIFFERENT

In what ways can those in other nations obey God rather than man when their leaders are corrupt and afflicting the people?

____

____

____

____

____

____

IGNORANCE IS CURRENCY FOR EVIL POLITICIANS TO STAY IN POWER

The word "ignorant" is an adjective that describes *a person in the state of being unaware, or even cognitive dissonance and other cognitive relation, and can describe individuals who are unaware of important information or facts*. Ignorance can appear in three different types: factual ignorance (absence of knowledge of some fact); object ignorance (unacquaintance with some object); and technical ignorance (absence of knowledge of how to do something).[1] Unfortunately, many are content to remain ignorant. The saying "ignorance is bliss" is so false and immature. We must be informed. Full of understanding, especially when it comes to the nation and what the Word means concerning corrupt leaders.

WHAT DOES NATIONAL REVIVAL LOOK LIKE?

Jonah 3:5-8 says, *"So the people of Nineveh believed God, proclaimed a fast, and put on sackcloth, from the greatest to the least of them. [6] Then word came to the king of Nineveh; and he arose from his throne and laid aside his robe, covered himself with sackcloth and sat in ashes. [7] And he caused it to be proclaimed and published throughout Nineveh by the decree of the king and his nobles, saying, Let neither man nor beast, herd nor flock, taste anything; do not let them eat, or drink water. 8 But let man and beast be covered with sackcloth, and cry mightily to God; yes, let every one turn from his evil way and from the violence that is in his hands."* The entire city of Nineveh repented and turned from its evil ways. Because of this, God refrained from bringing destruction upon these people. This is what revival looks like on a national level. What is hindering this type of revival from taking place today?

THE LORD'S DAY, JESUS REVEALS A GOVERNMENTAL CONFRONTATION THROUGH THE PROPHETIC EXPERIENCES OF JOHN

Jesus appeared to John the Revelator on the Lord's Day, the day that was designated for Emperor Domitian. How does this minister to you that the King of kings and Lord of lords gave a prophetic revelation to John on this particular day?

OUTGROWING THE YOKE IS ONE BIBLICAL WAY TO OVERCOME A WICKED RULERSHIP

PERSONAL REFLECTIONS

Every generation will face a corrupt leader, whether in their city, state, or nation. The job of believers is to grow in unity and walk in their God-given anointing. God desires His people to walk in the fullness of their calling. Once this happens, on an individual or corporate basis, the bondage of the yoke will be removed in three phases: 30-, 60-, and 100-fold. When someone reaches their 100-fold in their calling, nothing can bring them down again. Take this time with the Holy Spirit. Ask the Lord where you are in walking in all He has for you. If you feel like you are walking in bondage or under the pressure of those around you, what phase of breaking free are you in? Ask the Lord to help you reach your 100-fold. Write your prayer and what you hear Him say.

CHAPTER ELEVEN

The Restraining Force Holds the Antichrist Back Until the Rapture of the Church

SCRIPTURES

1. **Luke 21:8**—*And He said: "Take heed that you not be deceived. For many will come in My name, saying, 'I am He,' and, 'The time has drawn near.' Therefore do not go after them."*

2. **Matthew 24:11**—*Then many false prophets will rise up and deceive many.*

3. **Luke 21:9**—*But when you hear of wars and commotions, do not be terrified; for these things must come to pass first, but the end will not come immediately.*

4. **John 14:1**—*Let not your heart be troubled; you believe in God, believe also in Me.*

5. **Second Thessalonians 2:3-8**—*Let no one deceive you by any means; for that Day
will not come unless the falling away comes first, and the man of sin is revealed, the son of
perdition, 4 who opposes and exalts himself above all that is called God or that is worshiped,
so that he sits as God in the temple of God, showing himself that he is God. 5 Do you not
remember that when I was still with you I told you these things? 6 And* ***now you know what
is restraining****, that he may be revealed in his own time. 7 For the mystery of lawlessness is
already at work; only* ***He who now restrains will do so until He is taken out of the way****.
8 And then the lawless one will be revealed, whom the Lord will consume with the breath of
His mouth and destroy with the brightness of His coming.*

6. **Jude 1:9**—*Yet Michael the archangel, in contending with the devil, when he disputed about the body of Moses, dared not bring against him a reviling accusation, but said, "The Lord rebuke you!"*

7. **Revelation 12:7**—*And war broke out in heaven: Michael and his angels fought with the dragon; and the dragon and his angels fought.*

8. **Revelation 7:4-17**—*And I heard the number of those who were sealed. One hundred and forty-four thousand of all the tribes of the children of Israel were sealed:* [5] *of the tribe of Judah twelve thousand were sealed; of the tribe of Reuben twelve thousand were sealed; of the tribe of Gad twelve thousand were sealed;* [6] *of the tribe of Asher twelve thousand were sealed; of the tribe of Naphtali twelve thousand were sealed; of the tribe of Manasseh twelve thousand were sealed;* [7] *of the tribe of Simeon twelve thousand were sealed; of the tribe of Levi twelve thousand were sealed; of the tribe of Issachar twelve thousand were sealed;* [8] *of the tribe of Zebulun twelve thousand were sealed; of the tribe of Joseph twelve thousand were sealed; of the tribe of Benjamin twelve thousand were sealed.* [9] *After these things I looked, and behold, a great multitude which no one could number, of all nations, tribes, peoples, and tongues, standing before the throne and before the Lamb, clothed with white robes, with palm branches in their hands,* [10] *and crying out with a loud voice, saying, "Salvation belongs to our God who sits on the throne, and to the Lamb!"* [11] *All the angels stood around the throne and the elders and the four living creatures, and fell on their faces before the throne and worshiped God,* [12] *saying: "Amen! Blessing and glory and wisdom, thanksgiving and honor and power and might, be to our God forever and ever. Amen."* [13] *Then one of the elders answered, saying to me, "Who are these arrayed in white robes, and where did they come from?"* [14] *And I said to him, "Sir, you know." So he said to me, "These are the ones who come out of the great tribulation, and washed their robes and made them white in the blood of the Lamb.* [15] *Therefore they are before the throne of God, and serve Him day and night in His temple. And He who sits on the throne will dwell among them.* [16] *They shall neither hunger anymore nor thirst anymore; the sun shall not strike them, nor any heat;* [17] *for the Lamb who is in the midst of the throne will shepherd them and lead them to living fountains of waters. And God will wipe away every tear from their eyes."*

9. **John 6:44**—*No one can come to Me unless the Father who sent Me draws him; and I will raise him up at the last day.*

10. **Matthew 16:18**—*And I also say to you that you are Peter, and on this rock I will build My church, and the gates of Hades shall not prevail against it.*

11. **First John 4:17**—*Love has been perfected among us in this: that we may have boldness in the day of judgment; because as He is, so are we in this world.*

12. **First Thessalonians 4:16-18**—*For the Lord Himself will descend from heaven with a shout, with the voice of an archangel, and with the trumpet of God. And the dead in Christ will rise first.* [17] *Then we who are alive and remain shall be caught up together with them in the clouds to meet the Lord in the air. And thus we shall always be with the Lord.* [18] *Therefore comfort one another with these words.*

13. **Second Corinthians 12:2-4**—*I know a man in Christ who fourteen years ago—whether in the body I do not know, or whether out of the body I do not know, God knows—such a one was caught up to the third heaven.* [3] *And I know such a man—whether in the body or out of the body I do not know, God knows—* [4] *how* ***he was caught up*** *into Paradise and heard inexpressible words, which it is not lawful for a man to utter.*

14. **Revelation 12:5**—*She bore a male Child who was to rule all nations with a rod of iron. And her Child was* ***caught up*** *to God and His throne.*

15. **Matthew 11:12**—*And from the days of John the Baptist until now the kingdom of heaven suffers violence, and the violent* ***take it by force***.

16. **John 16:15**—*All things that the Father has are Mine. Therefore I said that* ***He will take of Mine*** *and declare it to you.*

17. **Acts 23:10**—*Now when there arose a great dissension, the commander, fearing lest Paul might be pulled to pieces by them, commanded the soldiers to go down and* ***take him by force*** *from among them, and bring him into the barracks.*

18. **First Corinthians 15:50-54**—*Now this I say, brethren, that flesh and blood cannot inherit the kingdom of God; nor does corruption inherit incorruption.* [51] *Behold, I tell you a mystery:* ***We shall not all sleep, but we shall all be changed***— [52] *in a moment, in the twinkling of an eye, at the last trumpet. For the trumpet will sound, and the dead will be raised incorruptible, and we shall be changed.* [53] *For this corruptible must put on incorruption, and this mortal must put on immortality.* [54] *So when this corruptible has put on incorruption, and this mortal has put on immortality, then shall be brought to pass the saying that is written: "Death is swallowed up in victory."*

19. **First John 3:2**—*Beloved, now we are children of God; and it has not yet been revealed what we shall be, but we know that when He is revealed,* ***we shall be like Him, for we shall see Him as He is***.

20. **Zechariah 14:3-4**—*Then the LORD will go forth and fight against those nations, as He fights in the day of battle. [4] And in that day His feet will stand on the Mount of Olives, which faces Jerusalem on the east. And the Mount of Olives shall be split in two, from east to west, making a very large valley; half of the mountain shall move toward the north and half of it toward the south.*

21. **Romans 14:10-12**—*But why do you judge your brother? Or why do you show contempt for your brother? For we shall all stand before the judgment seat of Christ. [11] For it is written: "As I live, says the LORD, every knee shall bow to Me, and every tongue shall confess to God." [12] So then each of us shall give account of himself to God.*

22. **Second Corinthians 5:10**—*For we must all appear before the judgment seat of Christ, that each one may receive the things done in the body, according to what he has done, whether good or bad.*

23. **First Corinthians 3:10-15**—*According to the grace of God which was given to me, as a wise master builder I have laid the foundation, and another builds on it. But let each one take heed how he builds on it. [11] For no other foundation can anyone lay than that which is laid, which is Jesus Christ. [12] Now if anyone builds on this foundation with gold, silver, precious stones, wood, hay, straw, [13] each one's work will become clear; for the Day will declare it, because it will be revealed by fire; and the fire will test each one's work, of what sort it is. [14] If anyone's work which he has built on it endures, he will receive a reward. [15] If anyone's work is burned, he will suffer loss; but he himself will be saved, yet so as through fire.*

24. **Revelation 19:7-9**—*"Let us be glad and rejoice and give Him glory, for the marriage of the Lamb has come, and His wife has made herself ready." [8] And to her it was granted to be arrayed in fine linen, clean and bright, for the fine linen is the righteous acts of the saints. [9] Then he said to me, "Write: 'Blessed are those who are called to the marriage supper of the Lamb!'" And he said to me, "These are the true sayings of God."*

25. **Isaiah 25:6**—*And in this mountain the LORD of hosts will make for all people a feast of choice pieces, a feast of wines on the lees, of fat things full of marrow, of well-refined wines on the lees.*

26. **Luke 21:36**—*Watch therefore, and pray always that you may be counted worthy to escape all these things that will come to pass, and to stand before the Son of Man.*

27. **Matthew 24:42**—*Watch therefore, for you do not know what hour your Lord is coming.*

28. **Matthew 25:1-13**—*Then the kingdom of heaven shall be likened to ten virgins who took their lamps and went out to meet the bridegroom. [2] Now five of them were wise, and five were foolish. [3] Those who were foolish took their lamps and took no oil with them, [4] but the wise took oil in their vessels with their lamps. [5] But while the bridegroom was delayed, they all slumbered and slept. [6] And at midnight a cry was heard: "Behold, the bridegroom is coming; go out to meet him!" [7] Then all those virgins arose and trimmed their lamps. [8] And the foolish said to the wise, "Give us some of your oil, for our lamps are going out." [9] But the wise answered, saying, "No, lest there should not be enough for us and you; but go rather to those who sell, and buy for yourselves." [10] And while they went to buy, the bridegroom came, and those who were ready went in with him to the wedding; and the door was shut. [11] Afterward the other virgins came also, saying, "Lord, Lord, open to us!" [12] But he answered and said, "Assuredly, I say to you, I do not know you." [13] Watch therefore, for you know neither the day nor the hour in which the Son of Man is coming.*

29. **Daniel 9:24-27**—*Seventy weeks are determined for your people and for your holy city, to finish the transgression, to make an end of sins, to make reconciliation for iniquity, to bring in everlasting righteousness, to seal up vision and prophecy, and to anoint the Most Holy. [25] Know therefore and understand, that from the going forth of the command to restore and build Jerusalem until Messiah the Prince, there shall be seven weeks and sixty-two weeks; the street shall be built again, and the wall, even in troublesome times. [26] And after the sixty-two weeks Messiah shall be cut off, but not for Himself; and the people of the prince who is to come shall destroy the city and the sanctuary. The end of it shall be with a flood, and till the end of the war desolations are determined. [27] Then he shall confirm a covenant with many for one week; but in the middle of the week He shall bring an end to sacrifice and offering, and on the wing of abominations shall be one who makes desolate, even until the consummation, which is determined, is poured out on the desolate.*

30. **Revelation 6:17**—*For the great day of His wrath has come, and who is able to stand?*

31. **Revelation 8–16**—*Due to the length of the text, please read from your Bible.*

32. **Matthew 24:29-31**—*Immediately after the tribulation of those days the sun will be darkened, and the moon will not give its light; the stars will fall from heaven, and the powers of the heavens will be shaken. [30] Then the sign of the Son of Man will appear in heaven, and then all the tribes of the earth will mourn, and they will see the Son of Man coming on the clouds of heaven with power and great glory. [31] And He will send His angels with a great sound of a trumpet, and they will gather together His elect from the four winds, from one end of heaven to the other.*

33. **Revelation 20:4-5**—*And I saw thrones, and they sat on them, and judgment was committed to them. Then I saw the souls of those who had been beheaded for their witness to Jesus and for the word of God, who had not worshiped the beast or his image, and had not received his mark on their foreheads or on their hands. And they lived and reigned with Christ for a thousand years.* [5] *But the rest of the dead did not live again until the thousand years were finished. This is the first resurrection.*

34. **Revelation 19:11-14**—*Now I saw heaven opened, and behold, a white horse. And He who sat on him was called Faithful and True, and in righteousness He judges and makes war.* [12] *His eyes were like a flame of fire, and on His head were many crowns. He had a name written that no one knew except Himself.* [13] *He was clothed with a robe dipped in blood, and His name is called The Word of God.* [14] *And the armies in heaven, clothed in fine linen, white and clean, followed Him on white horses.*

35. **Jude 1:14**—*Now Enoch, the seventh from Adam, prophesied about these men also, saying, "Behold, the Lord comes with ten thousands of His saints,"*

36. **Zechariah 14:5**—*Then you shall flee through My mountain valley, for the mountain valley shall reach to Azal. Yes, you shall flee as you fled from the earthquake in the days of Uzziah king of Judah. Thus the* LORD *my God will come, and all the saints with You.*

37. **First Thessalonians 5:9**—*For God did not appoint us to wrath, but to obtain salvation through our Lord Jesus Christ.*

38. **Revelation 3:10**—*Because you have kept My command to persevere, I also will keep you from the hour of trial which shall come upon the whole world, to test those who dwell on the earth.*

39. **Matthew 28:19**—*Go therefore and make disciples of all the nations, baptizing them in the name of the Father and of the Son and of the Holy Spirit.*

40. **Second Timothy 3:1-7**—*But know this, that in the last days perilous times will come: 2 For men will be lovers of themselves, lovers of money, boasters, proud, blasphemers, disobedient to parents, unthankful, unholy, 3 unloving, unforgiving, slanderers, without self-control, brutal, despisers of good,* [4] *traitors, headstrong, haughty, lovers of pleasure rather than lovers of God,* [5] *having a form of godliness but denying its power. And from such people turn away!* [6] *For of this sort are those who creep into households and make captives of gullible women loaded down with sins, led away by various lusts,* [7] *always learning and never able to come to the knowledge of the truth.*

41. **Second Thessalonians 2:1-12**—*Now, brethren, concerning the coming of our Lord Jesus Christ and our gathering together to Him, we ask you, [2] not to be soon shaken in mind or troubled, either by spirit or by word or by letter, as if from us, as though the day of Christ had come. [3] Let no one deceive you by any means; for that Day will not come unless the falling away comes first, and the man of sin is revealed, the son of perdition, [4] who opposes and exalts himself above all that is called God or that is worshiped, so that he sits as God in the temple of God, showing himself that he is God. [5] Do you not remember that when I was still with you I told you these things? [6] And now you know what is restraining, that he may be revealed in his own time. [7] For the mystery of lawlessness is already at work; only He who now restrains will do so until He is taken out of the way. [8] And then the lawless one will be revealed, whom the Lord will consume with the breath of His mouth and destroy with the brightness of His coming. [9] The coming of the lawless one is according to the working of Satan, with all power, signs, and lying wonders, [10] and with all unrighteous deception among those who perish, because they did not receive the love of the truth, that they might be saved. [11] And for this reason God will send them strong delusion, that they should believe the lie, [12] that they all may be condemned who did not believe the truth but had pleasure in unrighteousness.*

42. **Matthew 12:28-29**—*But if I cast out demons by the Spirit of God, surely the kingdom of God has come upon you. [29] Or how can one enter a strong man's house and plunder his goods, unless he first binds the strong man? And then he will plunder his house.*

43. **Ephesians 2:6**—*And raised us up together, and made us sit together in the heavenly places in Christ Jesus,*

44. **Colossians 2:15**—*Having disarmed principalities and powers, He made a public spectacle of them, triumphing over them in it.*

45. **Psalm 50:10**—*For every beast of the forest is Mine, and the cattle on a thousand hills.*

46. **First Peter 5:8**—*Be sober, be vigilant; because your adversary the devil walks about like a roaring lion, seeking whom he may devour.*

47. **Isaiah 11:6-9**—*The wolf also shall dwell with the lamb, the leopard shall lie down with the young goat, the calf and the young lion and the fatling together; and a little child shall lead them. [7] The cow and the bear shall graze; their young ones shall lie down together; and the lion shall eat straw like the ox. [8] The nursing child shall play by the cobra's hole, and the weaned child shall put his hand in the viper's den. [9] They shall not hurt nor destroy in all My holy mountain, for the earth shall be full of the knowledge of the* L*ORD* *as the waters cover the sea.*

48. **Zechariah 14:9, 16-19**—*And the LORD shall be King over all the earth. In that day it shall be—"The LORD is one," and His name one. ... [16] And it shall come to pass that everyone who is left of all the nations which came against Jerusalem shall go up from year to year to worship the King, the LORD of hosts, and to keep the Feast of Tabernacles. [17] And it shall be that whichever of the families of the earth do not come up to Jerusalem to worship the King, the LORD of hosts, on them there will be no rain. [18] If the family of Egypt will not come up and enter in, they shall have no rain; they shall receive the plague with which the LORD strikes the nations who do not come up to keep the Feast of Tabernacles. [19] This shall be the punishment of Egypt and the punishment of all the nations that do not come up to keep the Feast of Tabernacles.*

49. **Isaiah 65:20-25**—*"No more shall an infant from there live but a few days, nor an old man who has not fulfilled his days; for the child shall die one hundred years old, but the sinner being one hundred years old shall be accursed. [21] They shall build houses and inhabit them; they shall plant vineyards and eat their fruit. [22] They shall not build and another inhabit; they shall not plant and another eat; for as the days of a tree, so shall be the days of My people, and My elect shall long enjoy the work of their hands. [23] They shall not labor in vain, nor bring forth children for trouble; for they shall be the descendants of the blessed of the LORD, and their offspring with them. [24] It shall come to pass that before they call, I will answer; and while they are still speaking, I will hear. [25] The wolf and the lamb shall feed together, the lion shall eat straw like the ox, and dust shall be the serpent's food. They shall not hurt nor destroy in all My holy mountain," says the LORD.*

50. **Ezekiel 37:24-28**—*David My servant shall be king over them, and they shall all have one shepherd; they shall also walk in My judgments and observe My statutes, and do them. [25] Then they shall dwell in the land that I have given to Jacob My servant, where your fathers dwelt; and they shall dwell there, they, their children, and their children's children, forever; and My servant David shall be their prince forever. [26] Moreover I will make a covenant of peace with them, and it shall be an everlasting covenant with them; I will establish them and multiply them, and I will set My sanctuary in their midst forevermore. [27] My tabernacle also shall be with them; indeed I will be their God, and they shall be My people. [28] The nations also will know that I, the LORD, sanctify Israel, when My sanctuary is in their midst forevermore.*

51. **First Thessalonians 4:18**—*Therefore comfort one another with these words.*

52. **First Corinthians 15:51-52 KJV**—*Behold, I shew you a mystery; We shall not all sleep, but we shall all be changed, in a moment, in the twinkling of an eye, at the last trump: for the trumpet shall sound, and the dead shall be raised incorruptible, and we shall be changed.*

53. **Revelation 11:15-19**—*Then the seventh angel sounded: And there were loud voices in heaven, saying, "The kingdoms of this world have become the kingdoms of our Lord and of His Christ, and He shall reign forever and ever!" [16] And the twenty-four elders who sat before God on their thrones fell on their faces and worshiped God, [17] saying: "We give You thanks, O Lord God Almighty, the One who is and who was and who is to come, because You have taken Your great power and reigned. [18] The nations were angry, and Your wrath has come, and the time of the dead, that they should be judged, and that You should reward Your servants the prophets and the saints, and those who fear Your name, small and great, and should destroy those who destroy the earth." [19] Then the temple of God was opened in heaven, and the ark of His covenant was seen in His temple. And there were lightnings, noises, thunderings, an earthquake, and great hail.*

54. **Numbers 10:1-3**—*And the LORD spoke to Moses, saying: [2] "Make two silver trumpets for yourself; you shall make them of hammered work; you shall use them for calling the congregation and for directing the movement of the camps. [3] When they blow both of them, all the congregation shall gather before you at the door of the tabernacle of meeting."*

55. **Joel 2:1**—*Blow the trumpet in Zion, and sound an alarm in My holy mountain! Let all the inhabitants of the land tremble; for the day of the LORD is coming, for it is at hand:*

56. **Jeremiah 4:5-6**—*Declare in Judah and proclaim in Jerusalem, and say: "Blow the trumpet in the land; cry, 'Gather together,' and say, 'Assemble yourselves, and let us go into the fortified cities.' [6] Set up the standard toward Zion. Take refuge! Do not delay! For I will bring disaster from the north, and great destruction."*

57. **Matthew 24:3-14**—*Now as He sat on the Mount of Olives, the disciples came to Him privately, saying, "Tell us, when will these things be? And what will be the sign of Your coming, and of the end of the age?" [4] And Jesus answered and said to them: "Take heed that no one deceives you. [5] For many will come in My name, saying, 'I am the Christ,' and will deceive many. [6] And you will hear of wars and rumors of wars. See that you are not troubled; for all these things must come to pass, but the end is not yet. [7] For nation will rise against nation, and kingdom against kingdom. And there will be famines, pestilences, and earthquakes in various places. [8] All these are the beginning of sorrows. [9] Then they will deliver you up to tribulation and kill you, and you will be hated by all nations for My name's sake. [10] And then many will be offended, will betray one another, and will hate one another. [11] Then many false prophets will rise up and deceive many. [12] And because lawlessness will abound, the love of many will grow cold. [13] But he who endures to the end shall be saved. [14] And this gospel of the kingdom will be preached in all the world as a witness to all the nations, and then the end will come."*

58. **Luke 21:10-19**—*Then He said to them, "Nation will rise against nation, and kingdom against kingdom.* [11] *And there will be great earthquakes in various places, and famines and pestilences; and there will be fearful sights and great signs from heaven.* [12] *But before all these things, they will lay their hands on you and persecute you, delivering you up to the synagogues and prisons. You will be brought before kings and rulers for My name's sake.* [13] *But it will turn out for you as an occasion for testimony.* [14] *Therefore settle it in your hearts not to meditate beforehand on what you will answer;* [15] *for I will give you a mouth and wisdom which all your adversaries will not be able to contradict or resist.* [16] *You will be betrayed even by parents and brothers, relatives and friends; and they will put some of you to death.* [17] *And you will be hated by all for My name's sake.* [18] *But not a hair of your head shall be lost.* [19] *By your patience possess your souls."*

59. **Luke 19:13**—*So he called ten of his servants, delivered to them ten minas, and said to them, "**Do business till I come**."*

60. **Luke 19:13 KJV**—*And he called his ten servants, and delivered them ten pounds, and said unto them, **Occupy till I come**.*

61. **Romans 14:17**—*For the kingdom of God is not eating and drinking, but righteousness and peace and joy in the Holy Spirit.*

62. **John 14:27**—*Peace I leave with you, My peace I give to you; not as the world gives do I give to you. Let not your heart be troubled, neither let it be afraid.*

63. **Philippians 4:7**—*And the peace of God, which surpasses all understanding, will guard your hearts and minds through Christ Jesus.*

64. **Isaiah 55:12**—*For you shall go out with joy, and be led out with peace; the mountains and the hills shall break forth into singing before you, and all the trees of the field shall clap their hands.*

65. **Nehemiah 8:10**—*...Do not sorrow, for the joy of the LORD is your strength.*

66. **Psalm 85:8**—*I will hear what God the LORD will speak, for He will speak peace to His people and to His saints; but let them not turn back to folly.*

67. **Revelation 12:11**—*And they overcame him by the blood of the Lamb and by the word of their testimony, and they did not love their lives to the death.*

THE NUMBER OF PROPHECIES ABOUT THE FIRST AND SECOND COMING

It is fascinating that Jesus fulfilled more than 300 prophecies spoken about His birth, life, death, and resurrection. A study found the following information. The chance that any man might have lived down to the present time and fulfilled all eight prophecies is 1 in 10^{17} (1 in 100,000,000,000,000,000).[1] The fact that Jesus fulfilled hundreds of prophecies is statistically impossible apart from intelligent design, yet we know it was God Almighty who orchestrated each word in Scripture to bring about the coming of Jesus, our Messiah!

VAGABOND BELIEVERS WHO WANDER

Matthew 24:11 says, *"Then many false prophets will rise up and deceive many."* Notice the word "many." *Many* false prophets will rise, and *many* will be deceived. It would seem that believers should be able to identify a false prophet right away. However, according to this verse, that is not the case. Why do you think many will be deceived?

____

____

____

____

____

____

SEE THAT YOU ARE NOT TERRIFIED

Jesus knows how people process things. He understands that fear can come and bring terror to humanity. That is why He said many times, "Fear not," or "Do not be afraid." What steps should a believer take when fear comes?

____

____

____

____

____

____

THE RESTRAINING FORCE HOLDING BACK THE ANTICHRIST

There is a restraining force preventing the Antichrist from being revealed. Of the five points Rick Renner listed, which do you think is the reason for the Antichrist's delay?

WHAT IS THE RESTRAINER?

Why do you think that knowing the Church is the restrainer keeping the Antichrist from making his grand appearance should inspire boldness?

THE RAPTURE OF THE CHURCH

Although many believe the rapture isn't in the Bible, 1 Thessalonians 4:16-18 still describes an event where believers will be caught up and meet the Lord in the air. What are your thoughts on an actual Rapture occurring and the Church being taken away suddenly?

DURING THE RAPTURE WE WILL ALL BE CHANGED

In a twinkling of an eye, believers will meet Jesus and receive new bodies. Imagine all the pains, discomforts, deformities, and diseases completely eradicated, and a new, healthy, perfect, and glorious body becoming the new normal. It will be a wonderful experience, to say the least.

THE RAPTURE AND THE SECOND COMING

The Rapture is for the Church and will shock those who are left behind. It will be so sudden that confusion will spread worldwide. Ultimate panic will take over as people wonder what happened. The Second Coming will be different. It will be visible to all and will not cause confusion. People at that time will experience something completely different.

How do you think people who are left behind will respond after the Rapture?

____

____

____

____

____

____

LIST OF THE MAIN VIEWS ON THE TIMING OF THE RAPTURE OF THE CHURCH

For each theory about the timing of the Rapture, please share your thoughts. Was there anything new revealed to you? Why would you agree or disagree with that specific theory?

PRE-TRIBULATION RAPTURE

____

____

____

____

THE BEMA SEAT OF CHRIST

FOCUS POINT

During the Bema Seat, every believer will stand before God and give an account of all they did while on earth. Many of the things people have done will be consumed by fire. However, the costly things will be purified and come out even more beautiful than before. Take this time to examine your life. Take note of what you think would be burned and what would come out pure. This isn't about works and is not a works-based gospel. It's about time wasted on unimportant things and about rightsizing your life with the Bema Seat in mind. Write down what the Lord reveals to you.

MARRIAGE SUPPER OF THE LAMB

In most cultures, a wedding ceremony is celebrated with family and friends, the people who mean the most to the bride and groom. The Marriage Supper of the Lamb will be filled with everyone who means the most to the Lord, those who chose His Son while on earth. This feast will be so extravagant and filled with the masses. One can only imagine how many people will be in attendance. It will be a great multitude, for sure.

PARTIAL RAPTURE

MID-TRIBULATION RAPTURE

PRE-WRATH RAPTURE

POST-TRIBULATION RAPTURE

POST-MILLENNIAL THEORY

AMILLENNIALISM THEORY

COMFORT ONE ANOTHER

Jesus is coming for His Church. This is something every believer should be excited about. Fear should not be associated with the thought of the Rapture. Remember, information brings peace. Keep your eyes on Jesus and stay in the Word; these will bring you peace and comfort.

WHAT ABOUT THE LAST TRUMP?

Alan DiDio gave a very significant understanding of the last trump. What are your thoughts on the last trump, and how are you anticipating its sound?

ESCALATION BEFORE JESUS APPEARS

In Matthew 24 and Luke 21, Jesus shares with the disciples the signs of the end of the age. Throughout the list, Jesus reminds them in Matthew 24:13 that those who endure to the end will be saved. The Christian walk is one of enduring through all the trials, tribulations, and persecution. Our goal is to have endurance, stand on the Word, and not let fear enter our hearts and minds.

OCCUPY UNTIL HE COMES

As we wait for the Rapture to take place, we need to be occupied until Jesus comes. What does that look like for you, and how can you be about the Lord's business during this time?

____

____

____

____

____

____

THE WEAPON OF PEACE AND JOY

Jesus gave us guidance on what to look for in the last days and how to be prepared. As previously stated, information brings peace. Jesus is the peace we need. It doesn't stop there. He also gives joy. Why? Because He knows that fear and confusion will try to bring His people down. Thank God for Jesus and what He has provided for us, especially during times of uncertainty and hardship.

POWER TO STAND IN THE MIDST OF PURE MADNESS!

How many times have many preached about the Rapture with fear and trembling? Scaring people to get saved. For the believer, this shouldn't be the case. We should be ready and teach our kids that times will get rough, but we have the Savior who has prepared us with the proper tools to make it through what is coming before the Rapture. Have you experienced the fear-based teaching of the Rapture? If so, what has this chapter revealed to you that can help you walk in peace and joy?

____

____

IT IS OUR TIME TO STAND. BY THE POWER OF GOD, WE SHALL STAND!

PERSONAL REFLECTIONS

And they overcame him by the blood of the Lamb and by the word of their testimony, and they did not love their lives to the death.

—Revelation 12:11

As the Church prepares for the return of Jesus, it's vital for believers to understand that no matter what comes, the Church can overcome it all. How does this happen? By the blood of the Lamb, Jesus took care of that part, and "the word of their testimony" is our part.

It is important to use your mouth. Read the Word and make it your testimony. Use this time for personal reflection and find scriptures you can begin incorporating into your spoken testimony. Write them down and start speaking them today.

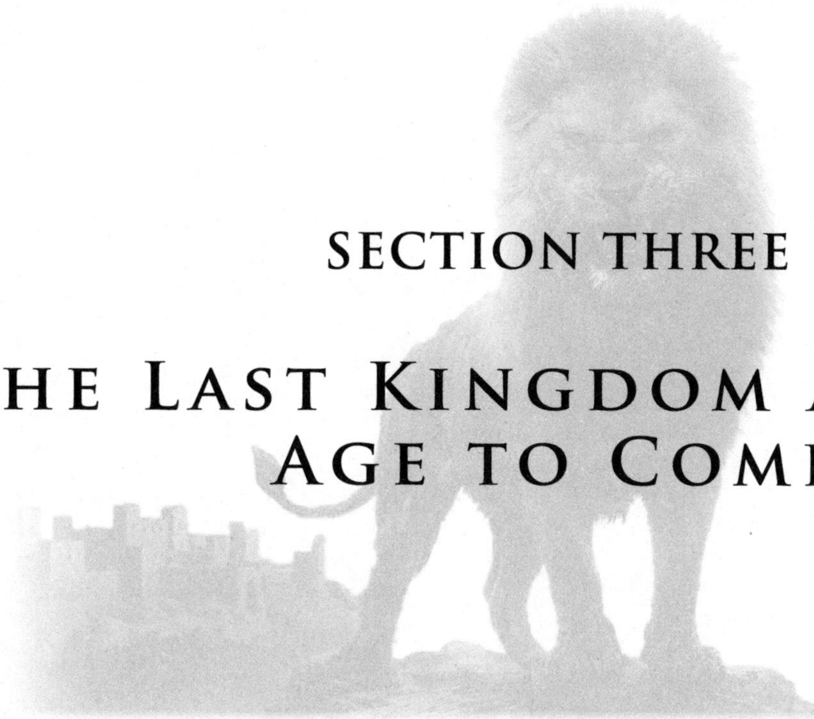

SECTION THREE

The Last Kingdom and the Age to Come

CHAPTER TWELVE

THE TWO BEAST KINGDOM

SCRIPTURES

1. **Revelation 13:1-2**—*Then I stood on the sand of the sea. And I saw a beast rising up
out of the sea, having seven heads and ten horns, and on his horns ten crowns, and on his
heads a blasphemous name.* [2] *Now the beast which I saw was like a leopard, his feet were like
the feet of a bear, and his mouth like the mouth of a lion. The dragon gave him his power, his
throne, and great authority.*

2. **Daniel 7:3-8**—*And four great beasts came up from the sea, each different from the other.*
[4] *The first was like a lion, and had eagle's wings. I watched till its wings were plucked off; and
it was lifted up from the earth and made to stand on two feet like a man, and a man's heart
was given to it.* [5] *"And suddenly another beast, a second, like a bear. It was raised up on one
side, and had three ribs in its mouth between its teeth. And they said thus to it: "Arise, devour
much flesh!"* [6] *After this I looked, and there was another, like a leopard, which had on its back
four wings of a bird. The beast also had four heads, and dominion was given to it.* [7] *After this
I saw in the night visions, and behold, a fourth beast, dreadful and terrible, exceedingly strong.
It had huge iron teeth; it was devouring, breaking in pieces, and trampling the residue with
its feet. It was different from all the beasts that were before it, and it had ten horns.* [8] *I was
considering the horns, and there was another horn, a little one, coming up among them, before
whom three of the first horns were plucked out by the roots. And there, in this horn, were eyes
like the eyes of a man, and a mouth speaking pompous words.*

3. **Revelation 13:3 KJV**—*And I saw one of his heads as it were wounded to death; and
his deadly wound was healed: and all the world wondered after the beast.*

4. **Zechariah 11:17 KJV**—*Woe to the idol shepherd that leaveth the flock! the sword shall be upon his arm, and upon his right eye: his arm shall be clean dried up, and his right eye shall be utterly darkened.*

5. **Revelation 13:12, 14**—*And he exercises all the authority of the first beast in his presence, and causes the earth and those who dwell in it to worship the first beast, whose deadly wound was healed. ...*[14] *And he deceives those who dwell on the earth by those signs which he was granted to do in the sight of the beast, telling those who dwell on the earth to make an image to the beast who was wounded by the sword and lived.*

6. **Revelation 13:4-6 KJV**—*And they worshipped the dragon which gave power unto the beast: and they worshipped the beast, saying, Who is like unto the beast? who is able to make war with him?* [5] *And there was given unto him a mouth speaking great things and blasphemies; and power was given unto him to continue forty and two months.* [6] *And he opened his mouth in blasphemy against God, to blaspheme his name, and his tabernacle, and them that dwell in heaven.*

7. **Daniel 7:25**—*He shall speak pompous words against the Most High, shall persecute the saints of the Most High, and shall intend to change times and law. Then the saints shall be given into his hand for a time and times and half a time.*

8. **Daniel 11:36-38**—*Then the king shall do according to his own will: he shall exalt and magnify himself above every god, shall speak blasphemies against the God of gods, and shall prosper till the wrath has been accomplished; for what has been determined shall be done.* [37] *He shall regard neither the God of his fathers nor the desire of women, nor regard any god; for he shall exalt himself above them all.* [38] *But in their place, he shall honor a god of fortresses; and a god which his fathers did not know he shall honor with gold and silver, with precious stones and pleasant things.*

9. **Second Thessalonians 2:4**—*Who opposes and exalts himself above all that is called God or that is worshiped, so that he sits as God in the temple of God, showing himself that he is God.*

10. **Ezekiel 28:2, 9-10**—*"Son of man, say to the prince of Tyre, 'Thus says the Lord God: "Because your heart is lifted up, and you say, 'I am a god, I sit in the seat of gods, in the midst of the seas,' yet you are a man, and not a god, though you set your heart as the heart of a god. ...* [9] *Will you still say before him who slays you, 'I am a god'? But you shall be a man, and not a god, in the hand of him who slays you.* [10] *You shall die the death of the uncircumcised by the hand of aliens; for I have spoken," says the Lord God.'"*

11. **Daniel 11:36-37**—*Then the king shall do according to his own will: he shall exalt and magnify himself above every god, shall speak blasphemies against the God of gods, and shall prosper till the wrath has been accomplished; for what has been determined shall be done.* [37] *He shall regard neither the God of his fathers nor the desire of women, nor regard any god; for he shall exalt himself above them all.*

12. **Psalm 55:20-21**—*He has put forth his hands against those who were at peace with him; he has broken his covenant.* [21] *The words of his mouth were smoother than butter, but war was in his heart; his words were softer than oil, yet they were drawn swords.*

13. **Revelation 13:7 KJV**—*And it was given unto him to make war with the saints, and to overcome them: and power was given him over all kindreds, and tongues, and nations.*

14. **Jeremiah 30:7**—*Alas! For that day is great, so that none is like it; and it is the time of Jacob's trouble, but he shall be saved out of it.*

15. **Daniel 7:21 NIV**—*As I watched, this horn was waging war against the holy people and defeating them.*

16. **Daniel 8:12 NIV**—*Because of rebellion, the LORD'S people and the daily sacrifice were given over to it. It prospered in everything it did, and truth was thrown to the ground.*

17. **Daniel 8:24 NIV**—*He will become very strong, but not by his own power. He will cause astounding devastation and will succeed in whatever he does. He will destroy those who are mighty, the holy people.*

18. **Daniel 11:31 NIV**—*His armed forces will rise up to desecrate the temple fortress and will abolish the daily sacrifice. Then they will set up the abomination that causes desolation.*

19. **Revelation 11:7 NIV**—*Now when they have finished their testimony, the beast that comes up from the Abyss will attack them, and overpower and kill them.*

20. **Matthew 16:18 NIV**—*And I tell you that you are Peter, and on this rock I will build* ***my church****, and* ***the gates of Hades will not overcome it****.*

21. **Matthew 11:11 NIV**—*Truly I tell you, among those born of women there has not risen anyone greater than John the Baptist; yet whoever is least in the kingdom of heaven is greater than he.*

22. **Revelation 13:8 KJV**—*And all that dwell upon the earth shall worship him, whose names are not written in the book of life of the Lamb slain from the foundation of the world.*

23. **Revelation 13:11**—*Then I saw another beast coming up out of the earth....*

24. **Revelation 13:13-14**—*He performs great signs, so that* ***he even makes fire come down from heaven*** *on the earth in the sight of men.* [14] *And* ***he deceives those who dwell on the earth by those signs*** *which he was granted to do in the sight of the beast, telling those who dwell on the earth to make an image to the beast who was wounded by the sword and lived.*

25. **Genesis 3:1**—*Now the serpent was more cunning than any beast of the field which the* LORD *God had made. And* ***he said to the woman****, "Has God indeed said, 'You shall not eat of every tree of the garden'?"*

26. **Second Corinthians 11:3**—*But I fear, lest somehow, as the serpent deceived Eve by his craftiness, so your minds may be corrupted from the simplicity that is in Christ.*

27. **John 5:43**—*I have come in My Father's name, and you do not* ***receive Me; if another comes in his own name****, him you will receive.*

28. **Revelation 13:12**—*And he exercises all the authority of the first beast in his presence, and causes the earth and those who dwell in it to worship the first beast, whose deadly wound was healed.*

29. **Second Thessalonians 2:9-11**—***The coming of the lawless one is according to the working of Satan, with all power, signs,*** *and* ***lying wonders****,* [10] *and with all unrighteous deception among those who perish, because they did not receive the love of the truth, that they might be saved.* [11] *And for this reason God will send them strong delusion, that they should believe the lie.*

30. **Exodus 7:11**—*But Pharaoh also called the wise men and the sorcerers; so the magicians of Egypt,* ***they also did in like manner with their enchantments.***

31. **Second Timothy 3:8**—*Now as Jannes and Jambres resisted Moses, so do these also resist the truth: men of corrupt minds, disapproved concerning the faith.*

32. **Revelation 13:15**—*He was granted power to give breath to the image of the beast, that the image of the beast should both speak and cause as many as would not worship the image of the beast to be killed.*

33. **Matthew 11:1-6**—*Now it came to pass, when Jesus finished commanding His twelve disciples, that He departed from there to teach and to preach in their cities.* [2] *And when John*

had heard in prison about the works of Christ, he sent two of his disciples [3] and said to Him, "Are You the Coming One, or do we look for another?" [4] Jesus answered and said to them, "Go and tell John the things which you hear and see: [5] The blind see and the lame walk; the lepers are cleansed and the deaf hear; the dead are raised up and the poor have the gospel preached to them. [6] And blessed is he who is not offended because of Me."

34. **John 20:29 NIV**—*Then Jesus told him, "Because you have seen me, you have believed; blessed are those who have not seen and yet have believed."*

35. **Matthew 12:38-39**—*Then some of the scribes and Pharisees answered, saying, "Teacher, we want to see a sign from You." [39] But He answered and said to them, "An evil and adulterous generation seeks after a sign, and no sign will be given to it except the sign of the prophet Jonah."*

36. **Daniel 3:1-7**—*Nebuchadnezzar the king made an image of gold, whose height was sixty cubits and its width six cubits. He set it up in the plain of Dura, in the province of Babylon. [2] And King Nebuchadnezzar sent word to gather together the satraps, the administrators, the governors, the counselors, the treasurers, the judges, the magistrates, and all the officials of the provinces, to come to the dedication of the image which King Nebuchadnezzar had set up. [3] So the satraps, the administrators, the governors, the counselors, the treasurers, the judges, the magistrates, and all the officials of the provinces gathered together for the dedication of the image that King Nebuchadnezzar had set up; and they stood before the image that Nebuchadnezzar had set up. [4] Then a herald cried aloud: "To you it is commanded, O peoples, nations, and languages, [5] that at the time you hear the sound of the horn, flute, harp, lyre, and psaltery, in symphony with all kinds of music, you shall fall down and worship the gold image that King Nebuchadnezzar has set up; [6] and whoever does not fall down and worship shall be cast immediately into the midst of a burning fiery furnace." [7] So at that time, when all the people heard the sound of the horn, flute, harp, and lyre, in symphony with all kinds of music, all the people, nations, and languages fell down and worshiped the gold image which King Nebuchadnezzar had set up.*

37. **Genesis 11**—*Due to the length of the text, please read from your Bible.*

38. **Revelation 14:9**—*Then a third angel followed them, saying with a loud voice, "If anyone worships* ***the beast and his image****, and receives his mark on his forehead or on his hand."*

39. **Revelation 14:11**—*And the smoke of their torment ascends forever and ever; and they have no rest day or night, who worship* ***the beast and his image****, and whoever receives the mark of his name.*

40. **Revelation 15:2**—*And I saw something like a sea of glass mingled with fire, and those who have the victory over the beast, over* ***his image*** *and over his mark and over the number of his name, standing on the sea of glass, having harps of God.*

41. **Revelation 16:2**—*So the first went and poured out his bowl upon the earth, and a foul and loathsome sore came upon the men who had the mark of the beast and those who worshiped* ***his image****.*

42. **Revelation 19:20**—*Then the beast was captured, and with him the false prophet who worked signs in his presence, by which he deceived those who received the mark of the beast and those who worshiped* ***his image****. These two were cast alive into the lake of fire burning with brimstone.*

43. **Revelation 13:15-18**—*He was granted power to give breath to the image of the beast, that the image of the beast should both speak and cause as many as would not worship the image of the beast to be killed.* [16] ***He causes all, both small and great, rich and poor, free and slave, to receive a mark on their right hand or on their foreheads,*** [17] *and that no one may buy or sell except one who has the mark or the name of the beast, or the number of his name.* [18] *Here is wisdom. Let him who has understanding calculate the number of the beast, for it is the number of a man: His number is 666.*

44. **Genesis 10:9**—*He was a mighty hunter before the LORD; therefore it is said, "Like Nimrod the mighty hunter before the LORD."*

45. **First Corinthians 15:45**—*And so it is written, "The first man Adam became a living being." The last Adam became a life-giving spirit.*

46. **Matthew 24:3-8**—*Now as He sat on the Mount of Olives, the disciples came to Him privately, saying, "Tell us, when will these things be? And what will be the sign of Your coming, and of the end of the age?"* [4] *And Jesus answered and said to them: "Take heed that no one deceives you.* [5] *For many will come in My name, saying, 'I am the Christ,' and will deceive many.* [6] *And you will hear of wars and rumors of wars. See that you are not troubled; for all these things must come to pass, but the end is not yet.* [7] *For nation will rise against nation, and kingdom against kingdom. And there will be famines, pestilences, and earthquakes in various places.* [8] *All these are the beginning of sorrows."*

47. **First John 2:18-27**—*Little children, it is the last hour; and as you have heard that* ***the Antichrist is coming****, even now* ***many antichrists have come****, by which we know that it is the last hour.* [19] *They went out from us, but they were not of us; for if they had been of us,*

they would have continued with us; but they went out that they might be made manifest, that none of them were of us. [20] *But you have an anointing from the Holy One, and you know all things.* [21] *I have not written to you because you do not know the truth, but because you know it, and that no lie is of the truth.* [22] *Who is a liar but he who denies that Jesus is the Christ? He is antichrist who denies the Father and the Son.* [23] *Whoever denies the Son does not have the Father either; he who acknowledges the Son has the Father also.* [24] *Therefore let that abide in you which you heard from the beginning. If what you heard from the beginning abides in you, you also will abide in the Son and in the Father.* [25] *And this is the promise that He has promised us—eternal life.* [26] *These things I have written to you concerning those who try to deceive you.* [27] *But the anointing which you have received from Him abides in you, and you do not need that anyone teach you; but as the same anointing teaches you concerning all things, and is true, and is not a lie, and just as it has taught you, you will abide in Him.*

48. **Revelation 7:4**—*And I heard the number of those who were sealed.* ***One hundred and forty-four thousand of all the tribes of the children of Israel were sealed.***

49. **Revelation 14:1**—*Then I looked, and behold, a Lamb standing on Mount Zion, and with Him* ***one hundred and forty-four thousand****, having His Father's name written on their foreheads.*

50. **Revelation 14:3**—*They sang as it were a new song before the throne, before the four living creatures, and the elders; and no one could learn that song except* ***the hundred and forty-four thousand who were redeemed from the earth.***

51. **Revelation 7:5-10**—*Of the tribe of Judah twelve thousand were sealed; of the tribe of Reuben twelve thousand were sealed; of the tribe of Gad twelve thousand were sealed;* [6] *of the tribe of Asher twelve thousand were sealed; of the tribe of Naphtali twelve thousand were sealed; of the tribe of Manasseh twelve thousand were sealed;* [7] *of the tribe of Simeon twelve thousand were sealed; of the tribe of Levi twelve thousand were sealed; of the tribe of Issachar twelve thousand were sealed;* [8] *of the tribe of Zebulun twelve thousand were sealed; of the tribe of Joseph twelve thousand were sealed; of the tribe of Benjamin twelve thousand were sealed.* [9] *After these things I looked, and behold, a great multitude which no one could number, of all nations, tribes, peoples, and tongues, standing before the throne and before the Lamb, clothed with white robes, with palm branches in their hands,* [10] *and crying out with a loud voice, saying, "Salvation belongs to our God who sits on the throne, and to the Lamb!"*

52. **Isaiah 44:5**—*One will say, "I am the LORD's"; another will call himself by the name of Jacob; another will write with his hand, "The LORD's," and name himself by the name of Israel.*

53. **Exodus 8:28**—*So Pharaoh said, "I will let you go, that you may sacrifice to the LORD your God in the wilderness; only you shall not go very far away. Intercede for me."*

54. **Exodus 9:4**—*And the LORD will make a difference between the livestock of Israel and the livestock of Egypt. So nothing shall die of all that belongs to the children of Israel.*

55. **Exodus 11:7**—*But against none of the children of Israel shall a dog move its tongue, against man or beast, that you may know that the LORD does make a difference between the Egyptians and Israel.*

56. **Genesis 4:15**—*And the LORD said to him, "Therefore, whoever kills Cain, vengeance shall be taken on him sevenfold." And the LORD set a mark on Cain, lest anyone finding him should kill him.*

57. **Isaiah 66:19**—*I will set a sign among them; and those among them who escape I will send to the nations: to Tarshish and Pul and Lud, who draw the bow, and Tubal and Javan, to the coastlands afar off who have not heard My fame nor seen My glory. And they shall declare My glory among the Gentiles.*

58. **Ezekiel 9:4-6**—*And the Lord said to him, "Go through the midst of the city, through the midst of Jerusalem, and put a mark on the foreheads of the men who sigh and cry over all the abominations that are done within it."* [5] *To the others He said in my hearing, "Go after him through the city and kill; do not let your eye spare, nor have any pity.* [6] *Utterly slay old and young men, maidens and little children and women; but do not come near anyone on whom is the mark; and begin at My sanctuary." So they began with the elders who were before the temple.*

59. **Exodus 13:9**—*It shall be as a sign to you on your hand and as a memorial between your eyes, that the LORD's law may be in your mouth; for with a strong hand the LORD has brought you out of Egypt.*

60. **Exodus 13:16**—*It shall be as a sign on your hand and as frontlets between your eyes, for by strength of hand the LORD brought us out of Egypt.*

61. **Exodus 28:38**—*So it shall be on Aaron's forehead, that Aaron may bear the iniquity of the holy things which the children of Israel hallow in all their holy gifts; and it shall always be on his forehead, that they may be accepted before the LORD.*

62. **Deuteronomy 6:8**—*You shall bind them as a sign on your hand, and they shall be as frontlets between your eyes.*

63. **Deuteronomy 11:18**—*Therefore you shall lay up these words of mine in your heart and in your soul, and bind them as a sign on your hand, and they shall be as frontlets between your eyes.*

64. **Zechariah 12:10**—*And I will pour on the house of David and on the inhabitants of Jerusalem the Spirit of grace and supplication; then they will look on Me whom they pierced. Yes, they will mourn for Him as one mourns for his only son, and grieve for Him as one grieves for a firstborn.*

65. **Romans 11:25-27**—*For I do not desire, brethren, that you should be ignorant of this mystery, lest you should be wise in your own opinion, that blindness in part has happened to Israel until the fullness of the Gentiles has come in. [26] And so all Israel will be saved, as it is written: "The Deliverer will come out of Zion, and He will turn away ungodliness from Jacob; [27] for this is My covenant with them, when I take away their sins."*

66. **Revelation 14:4**—*These are the ones who were not defiled with women, for they are virgins. These are the ones who follow the Lamb wherever He goes. These were redeemed from among men, being firstfruits to God and to the Lamb.*

THE FIRST BEAST RISING FROM THE SEA—THE ANTICHRIST

The book of Revelation is full of symbolism and prophetic insight into the end times. The First Beast is described as a vile creature no man has ever seen. When reading the description of this First Beast, how do you think Daniel and John felt as they penned it?

____

____

____

____

____

____

THE DEADLY HEAD WOUND TO THE BEAST, A GLOBALLY RECOGNIZED ASSASSINATION

The idea that a man of influence would be assassinated and then resurrected would affect many lives. This would truly be a miracle that could lead the masses into a deception unlike any other in history. What do you think the reaction to this scenario would be, and why do you think the devil would use this for his plan of destruction?

IS THE BEAST'S HEAD WOUND HIS BRAND?

It is an interesting thought that the head and the potential arm wound could encourage this Beast's followers to take the mark of the beast as a symbol of support. Like a branding, the masses would show up and present themselves as loyal to this Beast, taking the mark without knowing that it would set them apart for a horrific eternity.

THE CHURCH WILL NOT BE PRESENT AT THIS TIME

The Church knows what lies ahead and is aware of the Antichrist's schemes. If the Church were present at that time, there's no way we would stay silent and fail to call out the truth. What are your thoughts on this topic? Do you believe the *Ekklesia* will be present at that time? If so, why or why not?

THE WORLD WILL WORSHIP THE FIRST BEAST

FOCUS POINT

We live in a world that is all about experiences and awe-inspiring stories. Everything is on social media, and it's all about the views, likes, and shares.

It's hard to know what is real or fake anymore. In a time when AI is creating images and videos that appear to be real, people are gullible and falling for just about anything, even if it's absolutely ridiculous. Because of this, it would seem quite easy for a world to accept the Antichrist and all he offers because of a "miracle." With all this information, how should people stay innocent about the world wide web and social media fallacies to avoid deception?

HE WILL DEMAND TO BE WORSHIPED AS GOD

The Antichrist will be so full of evil and so deceived that he will believe himself to be God. Even though this is impossible, he still believes it and demands worship. Read Isaiah 14:13-14. How does the Antichrist mirror Lucifer in his thoughts and actions?

THE FIRST BEAST DECLARES HIMSELF AS GOD

An obvious red flag is when someone declares themselves a god. It would seem that people should call this out as false immediately. Unfortunately, that will not be the case at that time. Many will be deceived by this lie and succumb to the narrative set before them throughout the Tribulation.

SEXUAL PREFERENCE OF THE BEAST

It is possible that the Antichrist will be a homosexual. In a day and age when political correctness is pushed in every area, it would only make sense for this agenda to be pushed or used as a tool to win the approval of a carnal society. If it proves to be true that the Antichrist is a homosexual, what are your thoughts on why the Antichrist could use his potential sexual preference for his plan?

____

____

____

____

____

____

THIS BEAST WILL BE ACCEPTED BY ISRAEL ONLY TO BE BETRAYED BY HIM

Betrayal by someone once trusted can cause extreme pain and hardship. Imagine the reaction of those who sold out and gave their allegiance to the Beast, only to realize the deception was hidden in smooth words. When many in global society realize that the man of sin is hiding behind a façade, a shocking awareness may strike their hearts. Those who were asleep may suddenly awaken to the shock of having fallen for the guise of the greatest world figure ever known to man, now facing the consequences and the reality of what this means for their future. What do you think the response will be from those who come to the truth of the situation?

____

____

____

THE BEAST MAKES WAR AGAINST THE SAINTS

Those who become saints during the Tribulation will face great turmoil. The Antichrist will not only wage war against them but also overcome them. The persecution will be unlike any other time. Currently, we see this in specific locations; however, at that time, it will be worldwide. No one will be exempt. This is why it's so important to spread the gospel while we are still here on earth, to spare people from the intense evil of the Tribulation.

THE CHURCH HAS A DIFFERENT PROMISE THAN THE OLD TESTAMENT SAINTS AND THE SAINTS IN THE BOOK OF REVELATION

After reading this section, what distinguishes the Old Covenant, the *Ekklesia*, and the Tribulation saints?

THE SECOND BEAST RISING FROM THE EARTH—THE FALSE PROPHET

Have you ever noticed that when there is a corrupt leader, there is always a minion with influence who encourages people to trust that leader? Why do you think that is?

THE FALSE PROPHET WILL DISPLAY SIGNS AND WONDERS THAT EXCEEDS THE FIRST BEAST

Signs are used by the False Prophet and the Antichrist. People will always want a sign. We live in a "show me" culture, which echoes Jesus' time on earth. Read Matthew 12:38-39. The people asked Jesus for a sign. What was Jesus' response to this request?

HIS TWO HORNS AND HIS VOICE

The devil is a perverter of all things good. He knows that Jesus is the Lamb of God, which is why he uses the imagery of a lamb. However, this lamb will be full of deceit and darkness. This false messiah picture will lead people to believe a lie and to worship the Antichrist. He is not original and cannot create; this is why he perverts all that is good to advance his wicked agenda.

THE FALSE PROPHET WILL CAUSE THE WORLD TO WORSHIP THE ANTICHRIST

We know the First Beast will command the people's loyalty and dedication because of his miraculous resurrection. The Second Beast will gain enough notoriety through the signs and wonders he performs. With this in mind, why do you believe people will be so susceptible to deceit? What leads a culture to embrace such wickedness?

THE THIRD FIGURE IN THIS UNHOLY TRINITY—THE IMAGE OF THE BEAST GIVEN BREATH

As previously stated, people desire signs. Jesus, however, didn't need signs for authentication; prophecy served that purpose. Satan has had prophetic words spoken about him; however, his fate ends badly—the lake of fire. Because of this, he uses signs and wonders to deceive the masses, and he will do so during the Tribulation in such a way that many will be in awe and persuaded that the First Beast is a god.

A WARNING NOT TO BUILD YOUR FOUNDATION ON SIGNS AND WONDERS

In a previous question, you were asked to write what Jesus' response was in Matthew 12:38-39. An adulterous generation. Why do you think Jesus called those who sought a sign "adulterous"?

PARALLEL BETWEEN DANIEL 3 AND REVELATION 13 REGARDING THE IMAGE OF THE BEAST

Ecclesiastes 1:9 says, *"That which has been is what will be, that which is done is what will be done, and there is nothing new under the sun."* As seen in Genesis 11, Daniel 3, and several passages in Revelation, the spirit of Antichrist has been present from the very beginning. There is nothing new; what was will be done again. Our job is to be aware of this, identify that vile spirit, and until the Rapture of the Church, maintain our position that we will not be overcome by the gates of hell.

THE MARK OF THE BEAST

There are many speculations about what the mark of the Beast will be. What have you heard or been taught about what the mark is?

____

____

____

____

____

____

TAKING THE MARK IS AN ACT OF WORSHIP

Remember, at the beginning of the Tribulation, many will suddenly disappear in the Rapture. Those left behind will be gripped by fear and confusion about what happened. Leaders may convince the people that aliens took their loved ones. The Antichrist will come at the right time to offer peace and answers. As a result, many will be comforted and willing to accept whatever is presented to them. What they do not realize is that after the first half of the Tribulation, things will take a dramatic turn, and the fear they once knew will turn into extreme terror and anguish.

ARTIFICIAL INTELLIGENCE AND DIGITAL TRACKING

There have been false claims that the mark of the Beast is already here. However, this is not true. The mark will be required to buy food and for daily living. List some things that have been claimed to be the mark of the beast in our culture today.

____

____

____

____

____

____

THE SPIRIT OF ANTICHRIST IS ALIVE TODAY

The Church has the Word of God and the Holy Spirit to help identify those walking in the spirit of Antichrist. It is vital for the Church to be in the Word, in tune with the Holy Spirit, and aware of what is happening in the world. Unfortunately, many in the Church are unaware of what is taking place and are allowing evil to occupy high office and positions because they believe the Church shouldn't take part. As long as we are still here, we are to do our part to keep evil out of such positions and to confront the Antichrist spirit.

THE 144,000 JEWISH EVANGELISTS, WHO WILL PREACH THE GOSPEL DURING THE REIGN OF THE ANTICHRIST

Although those left behind didn't choose God before the Rapture, God, in His kindness, has a plan to bring the gospel to those alive during the Tribulation. What does this say to you about God and His great mercy?

____

____

____

____

____

____

THE 144,000 CARRY GOD'S MARK ON THEIR FOREHEADS

These servants of God will have a mark. It's interesting to note that, similar to this mark, the devil will impose his own mark. Again, this is proof that he is a copier and not an originator. This behavior reveals the jealousy he has toward God, and he can't help but copy and pervert.

THESE 144,000 MAY BE THE FIRST FRUITS OF A FUTURE REDEEMED ISRAEL

In light of the prophecy that God will raise 144,000 as "firstfruits" to stand for truth and righteousness during the Tribulation, how might this challenge your assumptions about the impact a single person or a minority can have in the face of opposition?

THE MACCABEES RESISTED OPPRESSIVE CULTURAL PRESSURE

In our culture today, have there been those with a similar makeup to the Maccabees? If so, list them on the lines provided.

THOSE WHO RESIST THE ANTICHRIST AND THE FALSE PROPHET

PERSONAL REFLECTIONS

This chapter revealed the two Beasts and their agendas during the Tribulation. Throughout history, many have risen to positions of authority and deceived the masses. Adolf Hitler is one example. He declared peace and claimed his actions were for the good of the people. Sadly, many believed him. In what ways should the believer be a voice for those who are easily deceived? What can you do to be a light and an example, ministering to the lost while we are still here? Take this time to write your answers and ask the Lord to speak to you. Write what you hear Him say.

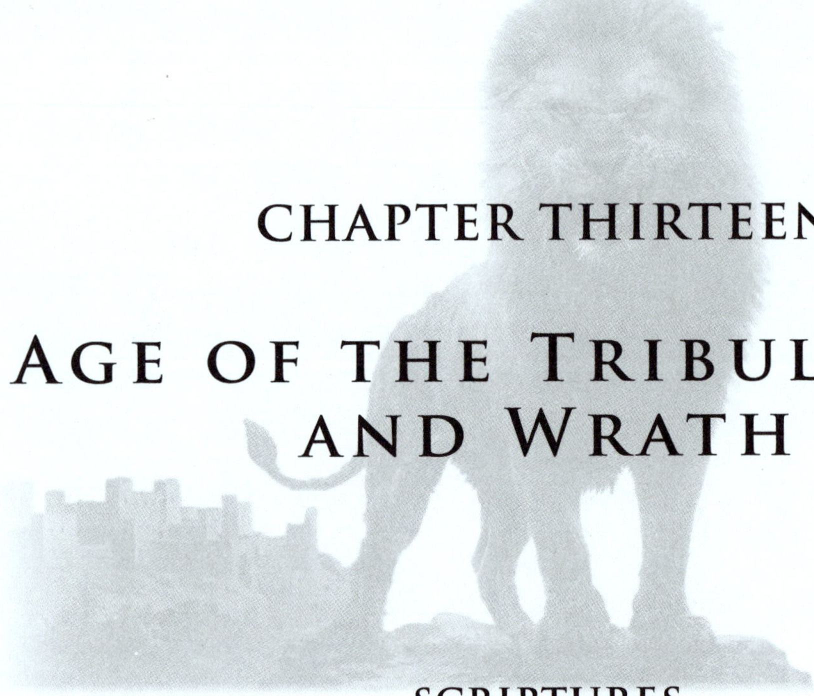

CHAPTER THIRTEEN

AGE OF THE TRIBULATION AND WRATH

SCRIPTURES

1. **Matthew 24:21-22**—*For then there will be great tribulation, such as has not been since the beginning of the world until this time, no, nor ever shall be.* [22] *And unless those days were shortened, no flesh would be saved; but for the elect's sake those days will be shortened.*

2. **Acts 2:17 KJV**—*And it shall come to pass in the last days, saith God, I will pour out of my Spirit upon all flesh: and your sons and your daughters shall prophesy, and your young men shall see visions, and your old men shall dream dreams.*

3. **First Thessalonians 5:9**—*For God did not appoint us to wrath, but to obtain salvation through our Lord Jesus Christ.*

4. **Second Thessalonians 2:6-7**—*And now you know what is restraining, that he may be revealed in his own time.* [7] *For the mystery of lawlessness is already at work; only He who now restrains will do so until He is taken out of the way.*

5. **Revelation 13:7 KJV**—*And it was given unto him to make war with the saints, and to overcome them: and power was given him over all kindreds, and tongues, and nations.*

6. **Matthew 16:18**—*And I also say to you that you are Peter, and on this rock I will build My church, and the gates of Hades shall not prevail against it.*

7. **First Thessalonians 4:16-17**—*For the Lord Himself will descend from heaven with a shout, with the voice of an archangel, and with the trumpet of God. And the dead in Christ*

will rise first. [17] *Then we who are alive and remain shall be caught up together with them in the clouds to meet the Lord in the air. And thus we shall always be with the Lord.*

8. **Acts 2**—*Due to the length of the text, please read from your Bible.*

9. **Acts 17:6 KJV**—*...These that have turned the world upside down...*

10. **Romans 11:26**—*And so all Israel will be saved, as it is written: "The Deliverer will come out of Zion, and He will turn away ungodliness from Jacob."*

11. **Isaiah 10:27**—*It shall come to pass in that day that his burden will be taken away from your shoulder, and his yoke from your neck, and the yoke will be destroyed because of the anointing oil.*

12. **Micah 4**—*Due to the length of the text, please read from your Bible.*

13. **Zechariah 13**—*Due to the length of the text, please read from your Bible.*

14. **Isaiah 2:17**—*The loftiness of man shall be bowed down, and the haughtiness of men shall be brought low; the LORD alone will be exalted in that day.*

15. **Jeremiah 30:3-7**—*"For behold, the days are coming," says the LORD, "that I will bring back from captivity My people Israel and Judah," says the LORD. "And I will cause them to return to the land that I gave to their fathers, and they shall possess it."* [4] *Now these are the words that the LORD spoke concerning Israel and Judah.* [5] *For thus says the LORD: "We have heard a voice of trembling, of fear, and not of peace.* [6] *Ask now, and see, whether a man is ever in labor with child? So why do I see every man with his hands on his loins like a woman in labor, and all faces turned pale?* [7] *Alas! For that day is great, so that none is like it; and it is the time of Jacob's trouble, but he shall be saved out of it."*

16. **Daniel 12:1**—*At that time Michael shall stand up, the great prince who stands watch over the sons of your people; and there shall be a time of trouble, such as never was since there was a nation, even to that time. And at that time your people shall be delivered, every one who is found written in the book.*

17. **Jeremiah 30:3-4**—*"For behold, the days are coming," says the LORD, "that I will bring back from captivity My people Israel and Judah," says the LORD. "And I will cause them to return to the land that I gave to their fathers, and they shall possess it."* [4] *Now these are the words that the LORD spoke concerning Israel and Judah.*

18. **Jeremiah 30:10-11**—*"Therefore do not fear, O My servant Jacob," says the LORD, "Nor be dismayed, O Israel; For behold, I will save you from afar, and your seed from the land of their captivity. Jacob shall return, have rest and be quiet, and no one shall make him afraid. [11] For I am with you," says the LORD, "to save you; though I make a full end of all nations where I have scattered you, yet I will not make a complete end of you. But I will correct you in justice, and will not let you go altogether unpunished."*

19. **Matthew 24:21**—*For then there will be great tribulation, such as has not been since the beginning of the world until this time, no, nor ever shall be.*

20. **Matthew 24:6-8**—*And you will hear of* ***wars and rumors of wars****. See that you are not troubled; for all these things must come to pass, but* ***the end is not yet****. [7] For* ***nation will rise against nation****, and* ***kingdom against kingdom****. And there will be* ***famines, pestilences****, and* ***earthquakes in various places****. [8] All these are the beginning of sorrows.*

21. **First Thessalonians 5:3**—*For when they say, "Peace and safety!" then sudden destruction comes upon them, as labor pains upon a pregnant woman. And they shall not escape.*

22. **First Thessalonians 4:13-18**—*But I do not want you to be ignorant, brethren, concerning those who have fallen asleep, lest you sorrow as others who have no hope. [14] For if we believe that Jesus died and rose again, even so God will bring with Him those who sleep in Jesus. [15] For this we say to you by the word of the Lord, that we who are alive and remain until the coming of the Lord will by no means precede those who are asleep. [16] For the Lord Himself will descend from heaven with a shout, with the voice of an archangel, and with the trumpet of God. And the dead in Christ will rise first. [17] Then we who are alive and remain shall be caught up together with them in the clouds to meet the Lord in the air. And thus we shall always be with the Lord. [18] Therefore comfort one another with these words.*

23. **Matthew 24**—*Due to the length of the text, please read from your Bible.*

24. **Revelation 6–12**—*Due to the length of the text, please read from your Bible.*

25. **Jeremiah 30:22**—*You shall be My people, and I will be your God.*

26. **Hosea 6:1-2**—*Come, and let us return to the LORD; for He has torn, but He will heal us; He has stricken, but He will bind us up. [2] After two days He will revive us; on the third day He will raise us up, that we may live in His sight.*

27. **Zechariah 12:10**—*And I will pour on the house of David and on the inhabitants of Jerusalem the Spirit of grace and supplication; then they will look on Me whom they pierced. Yes, they will mourn for Him as one mourns for his only son, and grieve for Him as one grieves for a firstborn.*

28. **Joel 2:32**—*And it shall come to pass that whoever calls on the name of the LORD shall be saved. For in Mount Zion and in Jerusalem there shall be deliverance, as the LORD has said, among the remnant whom the LORD calls.*

29. **Romans 10:13**—*For "whoever calls on the name of the LORD shall be saved."*

30. **Mark 13:19-20 NIV**—*Because those will be days of distress unequaled from the beginning, when God created the world, until now—and never to be equaled again. If the Lord had not cut short those days, no one would survive....*

31. **Daniel 9:24-27**—*Seventy weeks are determined for your people and for your holy city,
to finish the transgression, to make an end of sins, to make reconciliation for iniquity, to bring
in everlasting righteousness, to seal up vision and prophecy, and to anoint the Most Holy. 25
Know therefore and understand, that from the going forth of the command to restore and build
Jerusalem until Messiah the Prince, there shall be seven weeks and sixty-two weeks; the street
shall be built again, and the wall, even in troublesome times. 26 And after the sixty-two weeks
Messiah shall be cut off, but not for Himself; and the people of the prince who is to come shall
destroy the city and the sanctuary. The end of it shall be with a flood, and till the end of the
war desolations are determined. 27 Then he shall confirm a covenant with many for one week;
but in the middle of the week He shall bring an end to sacrifice and offering. And on the wing
of abominations shall be one who makes desolate, even until the consummation, which is determined, is poured out on the desolate.*

32. **Revelation 6:1-2**—*Now I saw when the Lamb opened one of the seals; and I heard
one of the four living creatures saying with a voice like thunder, "Come and see." 2 And I
looked, and behold, a white horse. He who sat on it had a bow; and a crown was given to him, and he went out conquering and to conquer.*

33. **Revelation 6:3-4**—*When He opened the second seal, I heard the second living creature
saying, "Come and see." 4 Another horse, fiery red, went out. And it was granted to the one who sat on it to take peace from the earth, and that people should kill one another; and there was given to him a great sword.*

34. **Revelation 6:5-6**—*When He opened the third seal, I heard the third living creature say, "Come and see." So I looked, and behold, a black horse, and he who sat on it had a pair of scales in his hand.* [6] *And I heard a voice in the midst of the four living creatures saying, "A quart of wheat for a denarius, and three quarts of barley for a denarius; and do not harm the oil and the wine."*

35. **Revelation 6:7-8**—*When He opened the fourth seal, I heard the voice of the fourth living creature saying, "Come and see."* [8] *So I looked, and behold, a pale horse. And the name of him who sat on it was Death, and Hades followed with him. And power was given to them over a fourth of the earth, to kill with sword, with hunger, with death, and by the beasts of the earth.*

36. **Revelation 6:9-11**—*When He opened the fifth seal, I saw under the altar the souls of those who had been slain for the word of God and for the testimony which they held.* [10] *And they cried with a loud voice, saying, "How long, O Lord, holy and true, until You judge and avenge our blood on those who dwell on the earth?"* [11] *Then a white robe was given to each of them; and it was said to them that they should rest a little while longer, until both the number of their fellow servants and their brethren, who would be killed as they were, was completed.*

37. **Revelation 6:12-17**—*I looked when He opened the sixth seal, and behold, there was a great earthquake; and the sun became black as sackcloth of hair, and the moon became like blood.* [13] *And the stars of heaven fell to the earth, as a fig tree drops its late figs when it is shaken by a mighty wind.* [14] *Then the sky receded as a scroll when it is rolled up, and every mountain and island was moved out of its place.* [15] *And the kings of the earth, the great men, the rich men, the commanders, the mighty men, every slave and every free man, hid themselves in the caves and in the rocks of the mountains,* [16] *and said to the mountains and rocks, "Fall on us and hide us from the face of Him who sits on the throne and from the wrath of the Lamb!* [17] *For the great day of His wrath has come, and who is able to stand?"*

38. **Revelation 8:1-5**—*When He opened the seventh seal, there was silence in heaven for about half an hour.* [2] *And I saw the seven angels who stand before God, and to them were given seven trumpets.* [3] *Then another angel, having a golden censer, came and stood at the altar. He was given much incense, that he should offer it with the prayers of all the saints upon the golden altar which was before the throne.* [4] *And the smoke of the incense, with the prayers of the saints, ascended before God from the angel's hand.* [5] *Then the angel took the censer, filled it with fire from the altar, and threw it to the earth. And there were noises, thunderings, lightnings, and an earthquake.*

39. **Habakkuk 2:20**—*The Lord is in his holy temple; let all the earth* ***keep silence*** *before him.*

40. **Revelation 8:7**—*The first angel sounded: And hail and fire followed, mingled with blood, and they were thrown to the earth. And a third of the trees were burned up, and all green grass was burned up.*

41. **Exodus 7:20**—*And Moses and Aaron did so, just as the LORD commanded. So he lifted up the rod and struck the waters that* ***were*** *in the river, in the sight of Pharaoh and in the sight of his servants. And all the waters that* ***were*** *in the river were turned to blood.*

42. **Exodus 9:23-25**—*And Moses stretched out his rod toward heaven; and the LORD sent thunder and hail, and fire darted to the ground. And the LORD rained hail on the land of Egypt.* [24] *So there was hail, and fire mingled with the hail, so very heavy that there was none like it in all the land of Egypt since it became a nation.* [25] *And the hail struck throughout the whole land of Egypt, all that* ***was*** *in the field, both man and beast; and the hail struck every herb of the field and broke every tree of the field.*

43. **Revelation 8:8-9**—*Then the second angel sounded: And something like a great mountain burning with fire was thrown into the sea, and a third of the sea became blood.* [9] *And a third of the living creatures in the sea died, and a third of the ships were destroyed.*

44. **Revelation 8:10-11**—*Then the third angel sounded: And a great star fell from heaven, burning like a torch, and it fell on a third of the rivers and on the springs of water.* [11] *The name of the star is Wormwood. A third of the waters became wormwood, and many men died from the water, because it was made bitter.*

45. **Revelation 8:12**—*Then the fourth angel sounded: And a third of the sun was struck, a third of the moon, and a third of the stars, so that a third of them were darkened. A third of the day did not shine, and likewise the night.*

46. **Joel 2:31**—*The sun shall be turned into darkness, and the moon into blood, before the coming of the great and awesome day of the LORD.*

47. **Matthew 24:29**—*Immediately after the tribulation of those days the sun will be darkened, and the moon will not give its light; the stars will fall from heaven, and the powers of the heavens will be shaken.*

48. **Revelation 8:13**—*And I looked, and I heard an angel flying through the midst of heaven, saying with a loud voice, "Woe, woe, woe to the inhabitants of the earth, because of the remaining blasts of the trumpet of the three angels who are about to sound!"*

49. **Revelation 9:1-12—***Then the fifth angel sounded: And I saw a star fallen from heaven to the earth. To him was given the key to the bottomless pit. 2 And he opened the bottomless pit, and smoke arose out of the pit like the smoke of a great furnace. So the sun and the air were darkened because of the smoke of the pit. 3 Then out of the smoke locusts came upon the earth. And to them was given power, as the scorpions of the earth have power. 4 They were commanded not to harm the grass of the earth, or any green thing, or any tree, but only those men who do not have the seal of God on their foreheads. 5 And they were not given authority to kill them, but to torment them for five months. Their torment was like the torment of a scorpion when it strikes a man. 6 In those days men will seek death and will not find it; they will desire to die, and death will flee from them. 7 The shape of the locusts was like horses prepared for battle. On their heads were crowns of something like gold, and their faces were like the faces of men. 8 They had hair like women's hair, and their teeth were like lions' teeth. 9 And they had breastplates like breastplates of iron, and the sound of their wings was like the sound of chariots with many horses running into battle. 10 They had tails like scorpions, and there were stings in their tails. Their power was to hurt men five months. 11 And they had as king over them the angel of the bottomless pit, whose name in Hebrew is Abaddon, but in Greek he has the name Apollyon. 12 One woe is past. Behold, still two more woes are coming after these things.*

50. **Revelation 9:13-21**—*Then the sixth angel sounded: And I heard a voice from the four horns of the golden altar which is before God, 14 saying to the sixth angel who had the trumpet, "Release the four angels who are bound at the great river Euphrates." 15 So the four angels, who had been prepared for the hour and day and month and year, were released to kill a third of mankind. 16 Now the number of the army of the horsemen was two hundred million; I heard the number of them. 17 And thus I saw the horses in the vision: those who sat on them had breastplates of fiery red, hyacinth blue, and sulfur yellow; and the heads of the horses were like the heads of lions; and out of their mouths came fire, smoke, and brimstone. 18 By these three plagues a third of mankind was killed—by the fire and the smoke and the brimstone which came out of their mouths. 19 For their power is in their mouth and in their tails; for their tails are like serpents, having heads; and with them they do harm. 20 But the rest of mankind, who were not killed by these plagues, did not repent of the works of their hands, that they should not worship demons, and idols of gold, silver, brass, stone, and wood, which can neither see nor hear nor walk. 21 And they did not repent of their murders or their sorceries or their sexual immorality or their thefts.*

51. **Revelation 11:15-19**—*Then the seventh angel sounded: And there were loud voices in heaven, saying, "The kingdoms of this world have become the kingdoms of our Lord and of His Christ, and He shall reign forever and ever!" [16] And the twenty-four elders who sat before God on their thrones fell on their faces and worshiped God, [17] saying: "We give You thanks, O Lord God Almighty, the One who is and who was and who is to come, because You have taken Your great power and reigned. [18] The nations were angry, and Your wrath has come, and the time of the dead, that they should be judged, and that You should reward Your servants the prophets and the saints, and those who fear Your name, small and great, and should destroy those who destroy the earth." [19] Then the temple of God was opened in heaven, and the ark of His covenant was seen in His temple. And there were lightnings, noises, thunderings, an earthquake, and great hail.*

52. **Revelation 15:7-8**—*Then one of the four living creatures gave to the seven angels seven golden bowls full of the wrath of God who lives forever and ever. [8] The temple was filled with smoke from the glory of God and from His power, and no one was able to enter the temple till the seven plagues of the seven angels were completed.*

53. **Revelation 16:2**—*So the first went and poured out his bowl upon the earth, and a foul and loathsome sore came upon the men who had the mark of the beast and those who worshiped his image.*

54. **Revelation 16:3**—*Then the second angel poured out his bowl on the sea, and it became blood as of a dead man; and every living creature in the sea died.*

55. **Revelation 16:4-7**—*Then the third angel poured out his bowl on the rivers and springs of water, and they became blood. [5] And I heard the angel of the waters saying: "You are righteous, O Lord, the One who is and who was and who is to be, because You have judged these things. [6] For they have shed the blood of saints and prophets, and You have given them blood to drink. For it is their just due." [7] And I heard another from the altar saying, "Even so, Lord God Almighty, true and righteous are Your judgments."*

56. **Revelation 16:8-9**—*Then the fourth angel poured out his bowl on the sun, and power was given to him to scorch men with fire. 9 And men were scorched with great heat, and they blasphemed the name of God who has power over these plagues; and they did not repent and give Him glory.*

57. **Revelation 16:10-11**—*Then the fifth angel poured out his bowl on the throne of the beast, and his kingdom became full of darkness; and they gnawed their tongues because of the*

pain. [11] *They blasphemed the God of heaven because of their pains and their sores, and did not repent of their deeds.*

58. **Revelation 16:12-16**—*Then the sixth angel poured out his bowl on the great river Euphrates, and its water was dried up, so that the way of the kings from the east might be prepared.* [13] *And I saw three unclean spirits like frogs coming out of the mouth of the dragon, out of the mouth of the beast, and out of the mouth of the false prophet.* [14] *For they are spirits of demons, performing signs, which go out to the kings of the earth and of the whole world, to gather them to the battle of that great day of God Almighty.* [15] *"Behold, I am coming as a thief. Blessed is he who watches, and keeps his garments, lest he walk naked and they see his shame."* [16] *And they gathered them together to the place called in Hebrew, Armageddon.*

59. **Revelation 16:17-21**—*Then the seventh angel poured out his bowl into the air, and a loud voice came out of the temple of heaven, from the throne, saying, "It is done!"* [18] *And there were noises and thunderings and lightnings; and there was a great earthquake, such a mighty and great earthquake as had not occurred since men were on the earth.* [19] *Now the great city was divided into three parts, and the cities of the nations fell. And great Babylon was remembered before God, to give her the cup of the wine of the fierceness of His wrath.* [20] *Then every island fled away, and the mountains were not found.* [21] *And great hail from heaven fell upon men, each hailstone about the weight of a talent. Men blasphemed God because of the plague of the hail, since that plague was exceedingly great.*

ARE WE IN THE END TIMES?

For the past 2,000 years, we have been in the last days. Currently, we would be in the last of the last days. The Church is the force that keeps the end times, or the Tribulation, from taking place. As long as we are here, we can continue the Great Commission and reach as many people with the gospel as possible.

THE CHURCH IS NOT APPOINTED FOR WRATH

As discussed in the previous chapter, opinions vary on whether and when the Rapture will occur. It's interesting to consider that some believe the Church will go through the Tribulation. Why do you think this is a position some take? Why would the Church experience God's unleashed wrath?

____

____

ARE WE ALREADY IN THE TRIBULATION?

Many believe we are in the Tribulation. How would you address this belief?

THE END OF THE CHURCH AGE IS THE BEGINNING OF THE AGE OF THE ANTICHRIST

The Church is the restraining force that is holding back the Tribulation, the Antichrist, and the False Prophet. If the Church were present during that time, our prayers would have an impact and help hold back the evil that is going to take place. This is why the *Ekklesia* needs to be removed: so the enemy's nefarious plans can be carried out, and the prophetic words spoken in Revelation fulfilled.

BEAST GIVEN POWER TO OVERCOME THE SAINTS

Those saved during the Tribulation will be overcome by the Beast. What is the difference between these saints and the *Ekklesia*?

THE *EKKLESIA* CANNOT BE OVERCOME!

FOCUS POINT

> *And I also say to you that you are Peter, and on this rock I will build My church, and the gates of Hades shall not prevail against it.*
>
> —Matthew 16:18

The Church has the strength, authority, and ability to overcome everything the enemy throws at it. We can push back the darkness. The gates of Hades, or hell, shall not prevail. "Prevail" means *to prove more powerful than opposing forces; to be victorious.*[1] According to this definition, Matthew 16:18 says that Hell will not be more powerful or victorious. This means the Church is the most powerful force and will always be victorious over the enemy and his schemes. Take this time to thank God for the authority He has equipped us with. Write down your prayer of thanks.

AGE OF GRACE

The body of Christ is present and holding back the darkness. This includes brothers and sisters in Christ around the world. The number of believers increases every day and will continue until the Church is taken away. At that point, the Age of Grace will end, and the Tribulation will begin.

BLOOD-BOUGHT BELIEVERS ARE BEAST-PROOF!

First Thessalonians 5:9 says, *"For God did not appoint us to wrath, but to obtain salvation through our Lord Jesus Christ."* Believers are not appointed to experience God's wrath. Instead, we are to obtain salvation through Jesus. The original Greek word for "salvation" is *soteria*, and in this verse it signifies *deliverance*, *preservation*, and *safety*.[2] When considering this verse and the definition of salvation, is this new to you? If so, write out your thoughts.

____

____

____

____

____

____

THE DAY OF THE LORD

Throughout history, God has been bound by His Word, the free will of humanity, and the systems in place. This means He couldn't step in and interfere to change the narrative. That narrative will change when the Tribulation begins. People alive at that time will experience God stepping in and not holding back. All the generations of difficulties have not faced anything close to what is coming. The Lord's Day will finally arrive, and He will not hold back. All the generations of wrath will come forth at that time.

BLESSINGS FOLLOW THE TIME OF JACOB'S TROUBLE

In Jeremiah 30:10-11, God says He will save Jacob and assures He will always be with him. This serves as a call to His children. He rescues us and remains present in our lives. Consider what this means to you personally and how it can serve as encouragement during challenging times. Write down your thoughts.

____

____

____

____

BIRTH PANGS LEADING UP TO THE TRIBULATION

Sometimes the global birth pangs are so severe that it seems as if the Rapture might occur at any moment. Throughout history, there have been periods when the Church likely felt the same way—times so tumultuous that they appeared to be the end times. The Holocaust was probably one such period. Can you think of other moments when people might have believed the same?

THE TIME OF JACOB'S TROUBLE REVEALS THE CHARACTER OF GOD WHO KEEPS HIS PROMISES

God desires that none should perish but that all be saved (*see* 2 Peter 3:9). Because of this, His mercy and kindness are revealed in keeping His promises. He is constant and remains faithful; if someone calls out to Him, repents of their sins, and believes in Jesus Christ, they are saved. Period. It's not a matter of "I hope I'm saved" or "maybe I will be saved." The answer is that you are saved. Thank God for the salvation available through Jesus.

DANIEL'S 70 WEEKS

The trials that will take place during the Tribulation will be so intense that God must shorten the days. How does this shortening of the days reveal God's mercy?

THE SEVEN SEALS OF THE TRIBULATION REVELATION 6–8

As you review the following seals that carry severe judgments against those on the earth during the Tribulation, take notes on your insights, anything that catches your attention in the scripture assigned to that section, and any other notable observations.

FIRST SEAL

SECOND SEAL

THIRD SEAL

FOURTH SEAL

FIFTH SEAL

SIXTH SEAL

SEVENTH SEAL

____

____

____

____

____

____

THE SEVEN TRUMPETS REVELATION 8–11

The seven seals brought severe judgments; however, the seven trumpets will be even more terrible. Jesus opened the seven seals, and the angels will sound the trumpets. Once again, as you read this section, take note of the key judgments with their assigned trumpet.

FIRST TRUMPET

____

____

____

____

____

____

SECOND TRUMPET

____

____

____

____

____

____

____

THIRD TRUMPET

FOURTH TRUMPET

FIFTH TRUMPET (FIRST WOE)

SIXTH TRUMPET (SECOND WOE)

SEVENTH TRUMPET (THIRD WOE)

THREE WOES COULD BE PART OF ONE MASSIVE EVENT— AN ASTEROID STRIKING EARTH

For those who believe we are currently living through the Tribulation, the fact that these judgments have not occurred shows that their understanding of that time is inaccurate. We have not seen these things take place. After reading through the seven seals and seven trumpets, how would you respond to someone who thinks we are in the Tribulation now?

THE SEVEN BOWLS REVELATION 15–16

Up to this point in the Tribulation, many intense and violent events will take place, yet those alive will have hard, blasphemous hearts. One would think the opposite would be true, that they would be begging God for forgiveness. Why do you think they will be so rebellious and refuse to turn from their sin, thus saving them from the wrath of God?

____

____

____

____

____

____

____

FIRST BOWL

Leviticus 13 discusses diseases affecting the skin or flesh. If someone had sores or boils, they were considered unclean and isolated. Those labeled unclean were not fit to enter God's presence. Imagine the separation and isolation they felt. This disease brought pain, rejection, and humiliation. Now look at the First Bowl; it brings a similar disease to every human who has taken the mark of the beast. They have chosen to follow deception and turn from God. The symbol of uncleanliness is evident in God's choice to pour His wrath on the skin in the First Bowl. He could be indicating that they will never enter His presence again. That's a strong understanding.

SECOND BOWL

It's a sad reality to imagine an ocean without any living creatures. The sin of the world will not only affect individuals but also animals. Another time in history when animals were affected was during the time of Noah. God flooded the earth, and every land animal not on the boat was killed.

THIRD BOWL

The Third Bowl is intended to make those who took the lives of saints and prophets understand the gravity of their actions. Genesis 4:10 says, "And He said, 'What have you done? The voice of your brother's blood cries out to Me from the ground.'" God has heard the cries of the martyred; and in this bowl, He will use blood as a judgment against those who murdered God's children. The Lord says, "Vengeance is Mine, I will repay" (*see* Romans 12:19). In this moment, vengeance will be His.

FOURTH BOWL

Up to this point, the most severe judgments have occurred, yet repentance is not in people's hearts. The opposite is true. A judgment of fire and heat brings bitterness, hatred, and rejection of God by the people. If they would only repent.

FIFTH BOWL

Imagine a pain so intense that people gnaw their tongues. This reaction is unknown to most today. The irrational behavior of these people shows that under such suffering, normal thinking goes out the window. There is no common sense, and during this time, no repentance. The only thing on their minds is fear, pain, and hatred.

SIXTH BOWL

With the removal of the river Euphrates, kings will be able to march and prepare for the war at Armageddon. The frog-like demonic spirits represent deception, filth, and moral corruption. The release of such a spirit shows that, up to this point, humanity hasn't faced all that the devil has to offer. The drying up of the river and the outpouring of these vile beings could prompt the leaders of that time to prepare for the epic battle. It may be that the people at this time are so sick of the judgments that they are ready to end it all.

SEVENTH BOWL

The Seventh and Final Bowl judgment represents the climactic outpouring of God's wrath upon an unrepentant world. When the angel pours his bowl into the air, a voice from the throne declares, "It is done!"—signaling the completion of divine judgment. What follows is unprecedented in human history: a catastrophic earthquake so massive that every island vanishes and every mountain crumbles, 100-pound hailstones crush every remaining structure, and plagues of unimaginable scale sweep across the earth. Yet the most sobering reality of this final judgment is not the sheer scale of destruction, but humanity's continued refusal to repent even in the face of total devastation—a posture that confirms the justice of the judgment itself. All of this sets the stage for the culminating event of the age: the Battle of Armageddon.

PERSONAL REFLECTIONS

Throughout the seven Bowls, God's intense wrath has been on full display. Up to this point, God has shown glimpses of His judgment in the Old Testament, but not to this extent. The Old Testament examples were minor in comparison. In the end, God will say, "It is done." John 19:30 says, "So when Jesus had received the sour wine, He said, 'It is finished!' And bowing His head, He gave up His spirit." The Father and the Son, after significant events, said similar phrases. When a statement like this is made, it signifies closure. No longer looking to the past but to the future. For Jesus, it meant looking ahead to a lost and dying world coming to salvation and to an eternity with Him. For God, it meant looking ahead to eternity, where all evil will be done away with and eternity will be as it was intended to be.

Take this time to reflect. Have you had a time in your life when you experienced pain, suffering, or even intense anger, and when it was over, you were able to breathe and move on? An "it is finished" moment? Write about it. How did you get through that time, and what has been the outcome? Ask the Lord to help you if you are currently in that situation. Remember, do each season well. Represent Jesus well. He will help and guide you through everything you are going through.

CHAPTER FOURTEEN

THE MOTHER OF ALL BATTLES: ARMAGEDDON

SCRIPTURES

1. **Jude 1:14-15**—*Now Enoch, the seventh from Adam, prophesied about these men also, saying, "Behold, the Lord comes with ten thousands of His saints,* [15] *to execute judgment on all, to convict all who are ungodly among them of all their ungodly deeds which they have committed in an ungodly way, and of all the harsh things which ungodly sinners have spoken against Him."*

2. **Revelation 16:12**—*Then the sixth angel poured out his bowl on the great river Euphrates, and its water was dried up, so that the way of the kings from the east might be prepared.*

3. **Revelation 16:13-16**—*And I saw three unclean spirits like frogs coming out of the mouth of the dragon, out of the mouth of the beast, and out of the mouth of the false prophet.*
[14] *For they are spirits of demons, performing signs, which go out to the kings of the earth and of the whole world, to gather them to the battle of that great day of God Almighty.* [15] *"Behold, I am coming as a thief. Blessed is he who watches, and keeps his garments, lest he walk naked and they see his shame."* [16] *And they gathered them together to the place called in Hebrew, Armageddon.*

4. **Revelation 19:11-18**—*Now I saw heaven opened, and behold, a white horse. And He who sat on him was called Faithful and True, and in righteousness He judges and makes war.* [12]
His eyes were like a flame of fire, and on His head were many crowns. He had a name written that no one knew except Himself. [13] *He was clothed with a robe dipped in blood, and His name is called The Word of God.* [14] *And the armies in heaven, clothed in fine linen, white and clean,*

followed Him on white horses. [15] *Now out of His mouth goes a sharp sword, that with it He should strike the nations. And He Himself will rule them with a rod of iron. He Himself treads the winepress of the fierceness and wrath of Almighty God.* [16] *And He has on His robe and on His thigh a name written: KING OF KINGS AND LORD OF LORDS.* [17] *Then I saw an angel standing in the sun; and he cried with a loud voice, saying to all the birds that fly in the midst of heaven, "Come and gather together for the supper of the great God,* [18] *that you may eat the flesh of kings, the flesh of captains, the flesh of mighty men, the flesh of horses and of those who sit on them, and the flesh of all people, free and slave, both small and great."*

5. **Colossians 2:14-15**—*Having wiped out the handwriting of requirements that was against us, which was contrary to us. And He has taken it out of the way, having nailed it to the cross.* [15] *Having disarmed principalities and powers, He made a* ***public spectacle*** *of them, triumphing over them in it.*

6. **Revelation 19:19-21**—*And I saw the beast, the kings of the earth, and their armies, gathered together to make war against Him who sat on the horse and against His army.* [20] ***Then the beast was captured****, and with him the false prophet who worked signs in his presence, by which he deceived those who received the mark of the beast and those who worshiped his image.* ***These two were cast alive into the lake of fire burning with brimstone****.* [21] *And the rest were killed with the sword which proceeded from the mouth of Him who sat on the horse. And all the birds were filled with their flesh.*

7. **Matthew 25:31-46**—*When the Son of Man comes in His glory, and all the holy angels with Him, then He will sit on the throne of His glory.* [32] ***All the nations will be gathered before Him, and He will separate them one from another, as a shepherd divides his sheep from the goats.*** [33] *And He will set the sheep on His right hand, but the goats on the left.* [34] *Then the King will say to those on His right hand, "Come, you blessed of My Father, inherit the kingdom prepared for you from the foundation of the world:* [35] *for I was hungry and you gave Me food; I was thirsty and you gave Me drink; I was a stranger and you took Me in;* [36] *I was naked and you clothed Me; I was sick and you visited Me; I was in prison and you came to Me."* [37] *Then the righteous will answer Him, saying, "Lord, when did we see You hungry and feed You, or thirsty and give You drink?* [38] *When did we see You a stranger and take You in, or naked and clothe You?* [39] *Or when did we see You sick, or in prison, and come to You?"* [40] *And the King will answer and say to them, "Assuredly, I say to you, inasmuch as you did it to one of the least of these My brethren, you did it to Me."* [41] *Then He will also say to those on the left hand, "Depart from Me, you cursed, into the everlasting fire prepared for the devil and his angels:* [42] *for I was hungry and you gave Me no food; I was thirsty and*

you gave Me no drink; [43] *I was a stranger and you did not take Me in, naked and you did not clothe Me, sick and in prison and you did not visit Me."* [44] *Then they also will answer Him, saying, "Lord, when did we see You hungry or thirsty or a stranger or naked or sick or in prison, and did not minister to You?"* [45] *Then He will answer them, saying, "Assuredly, I say to you, inasmuch as you did not do it to one of the least of these, you did not do it to Me.* [46] *And these will go away into everlasting punishment, but the righteous into eternal life."*

After God has poured out all His wrath, Jesus will come, ready for war. This is the ultimate handoff, the passing of the baton, so to speak. For His turn, He will not be alone but will come with an army of believers. Even if we won't be fighting this battle, the Lord may want us to witness the destruction of all evil at that time. What do you think that moment will feel like?

UNCLEAN SPIRITS RESEMBLING FROGS

These wicked creatures, whatever they may be, will be the devil's final effort to corrupt and deceive the masses. Given that the earth is full of demonic entities, why do you think they are held back until this very moment rather than roaming the earth now?

THE MOTHER OF ALL BATTLES

The world has faced many wars throughout history. Nations have risen against nations. No matter how terrible these wars have been, none will come close to the imagery of the Battle of Armageddon. Many lives were lost in previous wars; however, there were survivors on both sides of each war. Humanity has recovered and moved on. This will not be the case for those who enter this specific battle. Death and destruction are the fates of everyone on evil's side. No survivors will be present because those fighting the war will be the ones who took the mark of the beast and refused to repent during the judgments. The Bible says that there will be so much blood from this battle that it will reach the horses' bridles (*see* Revelation 14:20). Armageddon takes place in the valley of Megiddo. The total territory is 146 square miles. It's possible that this whole area will be full of the blood of those who were defeated by the sword of Jesus' mouth. That's a lot of blood.

IMAGINE THE SHOCK THESE ENEMIES WILL FEEL AS THEY REALIZE JESUS IS ABOUT TO ANNIHILATE THEM

After all is said and done, the First Beast (the Antichrist) and the Second Beast (the False Prophet) will be thrown into the lake of fire, where they will be tormented day and night forever. In such a short window, their actions were so evil that they will face their judgment for all eternity. When they are captured according to Scripture, what do you think the scenario will be like?

____

____

____

____

____

____

WHAT JESUS STARTED IN THE REALM OF THE SPIRIT HE WILL FINISH AT ARMAGEDDON

FOCUS POINT

When Jesus died on the cross, He made a way for the lost to be saved and guaranteed a future with Him for all eternity. This was a rescue mission. When He returns at Armageddon, it is another form of the same mission. He will not only defeat the enemy but also end all forms of torment for those who become believers during the Tribulation. Many will be persecuted at that time. Jesus will come and save those who are being persecuted. This shows that Jesus will always be merciful to those who call upon His name.

JESUS HUMILIATED HIS ENEMIES IN THE SPIRIT REALM— AT ARMAGEDDON, HE WILL PHYSICALLY DESTROY THEM

At the Battle of Armageddon, Jesus will finally defeat the enemy. Jesus has been present from the very beginning of time. He witnessed Lucifer as a beautiful angel, then being cast out of heaven, and all the evil he's ever committed on earth. One can imagine the anger Jesus felt toward the devil. After winning this battle, how would you feel if you were the one fighting, knowing that the devil would be locked up and the two Beasts would never harm people again?

____

____

____

____

____

____

WHAT IS THE LAKE OF FIRE?

The lake of fire is the eternal fate for the devil, his minions, the two Beasts, and every person who has denied Jesus as Lord. Hell will be swallowed up by the lake of fire, and it will be the place of eternal punishment. Not only is it a lake of fire that will burn those within it for all eternity, but the absence of the Father may be an even more intense judgment. Imagine never experiencing joy, love, peace, and everything else that God provides. Not only that, but also never experiencing the Holy Spirit and the presence of God. The thought of this is unimaginable for the believer. For the unbeliever, the suffering will last for all eternity. Let's win as many as we can for the Lord.

JUDGMENT OF THE SHEEP AND GOATS

During the Tribulation, people will still be able to repent and be saved. The number of those who do is unknown, especially since many will blaspheme God throughout all the judgments. There will still be those who do. Because of this, the saved and the unsaved will be separated at the end of the Tribulation. What do you think this moment will be like for those present?

____

____

____

____

____

____

THE SHEEP

The sheep are those who received Jesus as their Lord and Savior during the Tribulation. They will enter the Millennial Reign with their natural, physical bodies. Those who died during the Tribulation, the martyrs, will enter the Millennial Reign with spiritual bodies.

THE GOATS

PERSONAL REFLECTIONS

Throughout our lives, we will face opportunities to be the hands and feet of Jesus. Matthew 25:31-46 speaks of times when people can help those in need. We know we aren't saved by works because we are saved by what Jesus did, not by what we do. At the end of the Tribulation, those considered goats, who rejected Christ and didn't repent, will be cast immediately into the lake of fire. They will skip Hell and go directly to their eternal fate.

Here and now, we face daily choices that will shape our future. We are here to make a difference in the world. For some, there are many people to reach, while others have only a few. Even if it's one person at a time, that's still one person saved from an eternity of suffering and separation from God. Take this time to continue praying and interceding for the "one." Who is God speaking to you about today? Maybe someone is on the fence and needs that one contact and conversation to encourage them to change their life. People are one encounter away from being saved. Be that encounter, that encouragement. You can be the Jesus people need to meet to change their lives. Whoever God reveals to you, write it down and ask the Lord to give you a word for that person. Be faithful and send it to that person today.

CHAPTER FIFTEEN

MILLENNIAL REIGN: THE KINGDOM ON EARTH AS IT IS IN HEAVEN

SCRIPTURES

1. **Mark 14:62**—*Jesus said, "I am. And you will see the Son of Man sitting at the right hand of the Power, and coming with the clouds of heaven."*

2. **Luke 11:2-4**—*So He said to them, "When you pray, say: Our Father in heaven, hallowed be Your name. Your kingdom come. Your will be done on earth as it is in heaven. 3 Give us day by day our daily bread. 4 And forgive us our sins, for we also forgive everyone who is indebted to us. And do not lead us into temptation, but deliver us from the evil one."*

3. **Matthew 6:9-15**— *In this manner, therefore, pray: Our Father in heaven, hallowed be Your name. 10 Your kingdom come. Your will be done on earth as it is in heaven. 11 Give us this day our daily bread. 12 And forgive us our debts, as we forgive our debtors. 13 And do not lead us into temptation, but deliver us from the evil one. For Yours is the kingdom and the power and the glory forever. Amen. 14 For if you forgive men their trespasses, your heavenly Father will also forgive you. 15 But if you do not forgive men their trespasses, neither will your Father forgive your trespasses.*

4. **Revelation 20:1-3**—*Then I saw an angel coming down from heaven, having the key to the bottomless pit and a great chain in his hand. 2 He laid hold of the dragon, that serpent of old, who is the Devil and Satan, and bound him* ***for a thousand years****; 3 and he cast him into the bottomless pit, and shut him up, and set a seal on him, so that he should deceive the nations no more till the thousand years were finished. But after these things he must be released for a little while.*

5. **Ezekiel 40:4**—*And the man said to me, "Son of man, look with your eyes and hear with your ears, and fix your mind on everything I show you; for you were brought here so that I might show them to you. Declare to the house of Israel everything you see."*

6. **Ezekiel 40–48**—*Due to the length of the text, please read from your Bible.*

7. **Ezekiel 43:1-5**—*Afterward he brought me to the gate, the gate that faces toward the east. [2] And behold, the glory of the God of Israel came from the way of the east. His voice was like the sound of many waters; and the earth shone with His glory. [3] It was like the appearance of the vision which I saw—like the vision which I saw when I came to destroy the city. The visions were like the vision which I saw by the River Chebar; and I fell on my face. [4] And the glory of the LORD came into the temple by way of the gate which faces toward the east. [5] The Spirit lifted me up and brought me into the inner court; and behold, the glory of the LORD filled the temple.*

8. **Ezekiel 44:15-16, 23-24**—*"But the priests, the Levites, the sons of Zadok, who kept charge of My sanctuary when the children of Israel went astray from Me, they shall come near Me to minister to Me; and they shall stand before Me to offer to Me the fat and the blood," says the Lord GOD. [16] "They shall enter My sanctuary, and they shall come near My table to minister to Me, and they shall keep My charge.... [23] And they shall teach My people the difference between the holy and the unholy, and cause them to discern between the unclean and the clean. [24] In controversy they shall stand as judges, and judge it according to My judgments. They shall keep My laws and My statutes in all My appointed meetings, and they shall hallow My Sabbaths."*

9. **Ezekiel 43:18-27**—*And He said to me, "Son of man, thus says the Lord GOD: 'These are the ordinances for the altar on the day when it is made, for sacrificing burnt offerings on it, and for sprinkling blood on it. [19] You shall give a young bull for a sin offering to the priests, the Levites, who are of the seed of Zadok, who approach Me to minister to Me,' says the Lord GOD. [20] 'You shall take some of its blood and put it on the four horns of the altar, on the four corners of the ledge, and on the rim around it; thus you shall cleanse it and make atonement for it. [21] Then you shall also take the bull of the sin offering, and burn it in the appointed place of the temple, outside the sanctuary. [22] On the second day you shall offer a kid of the goats without blemish for a sin offering; and they shall cleanse the altar, as they cleansed it with the bull. [23] When you have finished cleansing it, you shall offer a young bull without blemish, and a ram from the flock without blemish. [24] When you offer them before the LORD, the priests shall throw salt on them, and they will offer them up as a burnt offering to the LORD. [25] Every day for seven days you shall prepare a goat for a sin offering; they shall also prepare a young bull*

and a ram from the flock, both without blemish. [26] *Seven days they shall make atonement for the altar and purify it, and so consecrate it.* [27] *When these days are over it shall be, on the eighth day and thereafter, that the priests shall offer your burnt offerings and your peace offerings on the altar; and I will accept you,' says the Lord GOD."*

10. **Zechariah 14:8-9**—*And in that day it shall be that living waters shall flow from Jerusalem, half of them toward the eastern sea and half of them toward the western sea; in both summer and winter it shall occur.* [9] *And the LORD shall be King over all the earth. In that day it shall be—"The LORD is one," and His name one.*

11. **Luke 1:32-33**—*He will be great, and will be called the Son of the Highest; and the Lord God will give Him the throne of His father David.* [33] *And He will reign over the house of Jacob forever, and of His kingdom there will be no end.*

12. **First Corinthians 15:25-27**—*For He must reign till He has put all enemies under His feet.* [26] *The last enemy that will be destroyed is death.* [27] *For "He has put all things under His feet." But when He says "all things are put under Him," it is evident that He who put all things under Him is excepted.*

13. **Revelation 19:16**—*And He has on His robe and on His thigh a name written:* KING OF KINGS AND LORD OF LORDS.

14. **Jeremiah 30:9 NIV**—*Instead, they will serve the LORD their God and David their king, whom I will raise up for them.*

15. **Ezekiel 34:23-24 NIV**— *I will place over them one shepherd, my servant David, and he will tend them; he will tend them and be their shepherd.* [24] *I the LORD will be their God, and my servant David will be prince among them. I the LORD have spoken.*

16. **Ezekiel 37:24-25**—*David My servant shall be king over them, and they shall all have one shepherd; they shall also walk in My judgments and observe My statutes, and do them.* [25] *Then they shall dwell in the land that I have given to Jacob My servant, where your fathers dwelt; and they shall dwell there, they, their children, and their children's children, forever; and My servant David shall be their prince forever.*

17. **Hosea 3:5**—*Afterward the children of Israel shall return and seek the LORD their God and David their king. They shall fear the LORD and His goodness in the latter days.*

18. **Second Samuel 7:16**—*And your house and your kingdom shall be established forever before you. Your throne shall be established forever.*

19. **Daniel 7:22, 27**—*Until the Ancient of Days came, and a judgment was made in favor of the saints of the Most High, and the time came for the saints to possess the kingdom. …* [27] *Then the kingdom and dominion, and the greatness of the kingdoms under the whole heaven, shall be given to the people, the saints of the Most High. His kingdom is an everlasting kingdom, and all dominions shall serve and obey Him.*

20. **First Corinthians 6:2**—*Do you not know that the* ***saints will judge the world****? And if the world will be judged by you, are you unworthy to judge the smallest matters?*

21. **Revelation 20:4-6**—*And I saw thrones, and they sat on them, and judgment was committed to them. Then I saw the souls of those who had been beheaded for their witness to Jesus and for the word of God, who had not worshiped the beast or his image, and had not received his mark on their foreheads or on their hands.* ***And they lived and reigned with Christ for a thousand years.*** [5] *But the rest of the dead did not live again until the thousand years were finished. This is the first resurrection.* [6] *Blessed and holy is he who has part in the first resurrection. Over such the second death has no power, but they shall be priests of God and of Christ, and* ***shall reign with Him a thousand years.***

22. **First Corinthians 15:36**—*Foolish one, what you sow is not made alive unless it dies.*

23. **Luke 19:12-27**—*Therefore He said: "A certain nobleman went into a far country to receive for himself a kingdom and to return.* [13] *So he called ten of his servants, delivered to them ten minas, and said to them, 'Do business till I come.'* [14] *But his citizens hated him, and sent a delegation after him, saying, 'We will not have this man to reign over us.'* [15] *And so it was that when he returned, having received the kingdom, he then commanded these servants, to whom he had given the money, to be called to him, that he might know how much every man had gained by trading.* [16] *Then came the first, saying, 'Master, your mina has earned ten minas.'* [17] *And he said to him, 'Well done, good servant; because you were faithful in a very little, have authority over ten cities.'* [18] *And the second came, saying, 'Master, your mina has earned five minas.'* [19] *Likewise he said to him, 'You also be over five cities.'* [20] *Then another came, saying, 'Master, here is your mina, which I have kept put away in a handkerchief.* [21] *For I feared you, because you are an austere man. You collect what you did not deposit, and reap what you did not sow.'* [22] *And he said to him, 'Out of your own mouth I will judge you, you wicked servant. You knew that I was an austere man, collecting what I did not deposit and reaping what I did not sow.* [23] *Why then did you not put my money in the bank, that at my coming I might have collected it with interest?'* [24] *And he said to those who stood by, 'Take the mina from him, and give it to him who has ten minas.'* [25] *(But they said to him, 'Master, he has ten minas.')* [26] *'For I say to you, that to everyone who has will be given; and from him who does not have, even*

what he has will be taken away from him. [27] *But bring here those enemies of mine, who did not want me to reign over them, and slay them before me.'"*

24. **Matthew 25:14-30**—*For the kingdom of heaven is like a man traveling to a far country, who called his own servants and delivered his goods to them.* [15] *And to one he gave five talents, to another two, and to another one, to each according to his own ability; and immediately he went on a journey.* [16] *Then he who had received the five talents went and traded with them, and made another five talents.* [17] *And likewise he who had received two gained two more also.* [18] *But he who had received one went and dug in the ground, and hid his lord's money.* [19] *After a long time the lord of those servants came and settled accounts with them.* [20] *So he who had received five talents came and brought five other talents, saying, "Lord, you delivered to me five talents; look, I have gained five more talents besides them."* [21] *His lord said to him, "Well done, good and faithful servant; you were faithful over a few things, I will make you ruler over many things. Enter into the joy of your lord."* [22] *He also who had received two talents came and said, "Lord, you delivered to me two talents; look, I have gained two more talents besides them."* [23] *His lord said to him, "Well done, good and faithful servant; you have been faithful over a few things, I will make you ruler over many things. Enter into the joy of your lord."* [24] *Then he who had received the one talent came and said, "Lord, I knew you to be a hard man, reaping where you have not sown, and gathering where you have not scattered seed.* [25] *And I was afraid, and went and hid your talent in the ground. Look, there you have what is yours."* [26] *But his lord answered and said to him, "You wicked and lazy servant, you knew that I reap where I have not sown, and gather where I have not scattered seed.* [27] *So you ought to have deposited my money with the bankers, and at my coming I would have received back my own with interest.* [28] *So take the talent from him, and give it to him who has ten talents.* [29] *'For to everyone who has, more will be given, and he will have abundance; but from him who does not have, even what he has will be taken away.* [30] *And cast the unprofitable servant into the outer darkness. There will be weeping and gnashing of teeth.'"*

25. **Revelation 20:6**—*...but they shall be **priests** of God and of Christ, and shall reign with Him a thousand years.*

26. **Revelation 5:10**—*And have made us **kings** and **priests** to our God; and we shall reign on the earth.*

27. **Revelation 1:6**—*and has made us kings and priests to His God and Father, to Him be glory and dominion forever and ever. Amen.*

28. **Isaiah 65:20**—*No more shall an infant from there live but a few days, nor an old man who has not fulfilled his days; for the child shall die one hundred years old, but the sinner being one hundred years old shall be accursed.*

29. **Isaiah 11:9**—*They shall not hurt nor destroy in all My holy mountain, for the earth shall be full of the knowledge of the LORD as the waters cover the sea.*

30. **Jeremiah 31:34**—*No more shall every man teach his neighbor, and every man his brother, saying, "Know the LORD," for they all shall know Me, from the least of them to the greatest of them, says the LORD. For I will forgive their iniquity, and their sin I will remember no more.*

31. **Habakkuk 2:14**—*For the earth will be filled with the knowledge of the glory of the LORD, as the waters cover the sea.*

32. **Zechariah 14:16**—*And it shall come to pass that everyone who is left of all the nations which came against Jerusalem shall go up from year to year to worship the King, the LORD of hosts, and to keep the Feast of Tabernacles.*

33. **Isaiah 2:2-3**—*Now it shall come to pass in the latter days that the mountain of the LORD's house shall be established on the top of the mountains, and shall be exalted above the hills; and all nations shall flow to it.* [3] *Many people shall come and say, "Come, and let us go up to the mountain of the LORD, to the house of the God of Jacob; He will teach us His ways, and we shall walk in His paths." For out of Zion shall go forth the law, and the word of the LORD from Jerusalem.*

34. **Zechariah 8:20-23**—*Thus says the LORD of hosts: "Peoples shall yet come, inhabitants of many cities;* [21] *the inhabitants of one city shall go to another, saying, 'Let us continue to go and pray before the LORD, and seek the LORD of hosts. I myself will go also.'* [22] *Yes, many peoples and strong nations shall come to seek the LORD of hosts in Jerusalem, and to pray before the LORD."* [23] *Thus says the LORD of hosts: "In those days ten men from every language of the nations shall grasp the sleeve of a Jewish man, saying, 'Let us go with you, for we have heard that God is with you.'"*

35. **Ezekiel 43**—*Due to the length of the text, please read from your Bible.*

36. **Zechariah 14:20-21**—*In that day "HOLINESS TO THE LORD" shall be engraved on the bells of the horses. The pots in the LORD's house shall be like the bowls before the altar.* [21] *Yes, every pot in Jerusalem and Judah shall be holiness to the LORD of hosts. Everyone who sacrifices shall come and take them and cook in them. In that day there shall no longer be a Canaanite in the house of the LORD of hosts.*

37. **Zechariah 14:17-19**—*And it shall be that whichever of the families of the earth do not come up to Jerusalem to worship the King, the LORD of hosts, on them there will be no*

rain. [18] *If the family of Egypt will not come up and enter in, they shall have no rain; they shall receive the plague with which the* L*ORD strikes the nations who do not come up to keep the Feast of Tabernacles.* [19] *This shall be the punishment of Egypt and the punishment of all the nations that do not come up to keep the Feast of Tabernacles.*

38. **Isaiah 65:17-19**—*For behold, I create new heavens and a new earth; and the former shall not be remembered or come to mind.* [18] *But be glad and rejoice forever in what I create; for behold, I create Jerusalem as a rejoicing, and her people a joy.* [19] *I will rejoice in Jerusalem, and joy in My people; the voice of weeping shall no longer be heard in her, nor the voice of crying.*

39. **Revelation 21**—*Due to the length of the text, please read from your Bible.*

40. **Isaiah 65:20**—*No more shall an infant from there live but a few days, nor an old man who has not fulfilled his days; for the child shall die one hundred years old, but the sinner being one hundred years old shall be accursed.*

41. **Isaiah 65:21-24**—*They shall build houses and inhabit them; they shall plant vineyards and eat their fruit.* [22] *They shall not build and another inhabit; they shall not plant and another eat; for as the days of a tree, so shall be the days of My people, and My elect shall long enjoy the work of their hands.* [23] *They shall not labor in vain, nor bring forth children for trouble; for they shall be the descendants of the blessed of the* L*ORD, and their offspring with them.* [24] *It shall come to pass that before they call, I will answer; and while they are still speaking, I will hear.*

42. **Isaiah 11:6-8**—*The wolf also shall dwell with the lamb, the leopard shall lie down with the young goat, the calf and the young lion and the fatling together; and a little child shall lead them.* [7] *The cow and the bear shall graze; their young ones shall lie down together; and the lion shall eat straw like the ox.* [8] *The nursing child shall play by the cobra's hole, and the weaned child shall put his hand in the viper's den.*

43. **Isaiah 65:25**—*"The wolf and the lamb shall feed together, the lion shall eat straw like the ox, and dust shall be the serpent's food. They shall not hurt nor destroy in all My holy mountain," says the* L*ORD.*

44. **Revelation 20:7-8**—*Now when the thousand years have expired, Satan will be released from his prison* [8] *and will go out to deceive the nations which are in the four corners of the earth, Gog and Magog, to gather them together to battle, whose number is as the sand of the sea.*

45. **Matthew 24:22**—*And unless those days were shortened, no flesh would be saved; but for the elect's sake those days will be shortened.*

46. **Revelation 20:3**—*And he cast him into the bottomless pit, and shut him up, and set a seal on him, so that he should deceive the nations no more till the thousand years were finished. But after these things he must be released for a little while.*

47. **Revelation 20:9**—*They went up on the breadth of the earth and surrounded the camp of the saints and the beloved city. And fire came down from God out of heaven and devoured them.*

48. **Revelation 20:10**—*The devil, who deceived them, was cast into the lake of fire and brimstone where the beast and the false prophet are. And they will be tormented day and night forever and ever.*

49. **Revelation 20:11-15**—*Then I saw* ***a great white throne*** *and Him who sat on it, from whose face the earth and the heaven fled away. And there was found no place for them.*
[12] ***And I saw the dead, small and great, standing before God, and books were opened****.*
And another book was opened, which is the Book of Life. And the dead were judged according to their works, by the things which were written in the books. [13] *The sea gave up the dead who were in it, and Death and Hades delivered up the dead who were in them. And* ***they were judged, each one according to his works.*** [14] ***Then Death and Hades were cast into the lake of fire. This is the second death****.* [15] ***And anyone not found written in the Book of Life was cast into the lake of fire.***

After the goats and sheep are separated, the Millennial Reign will begin. Up to this point, the world has not known peace. Those who survived the Tribulation will breathe easily, no longer fearing for their lives as they did during the persecution and judgments they just endured. They will join those returning with Jesus at the Second Coming. Imagine what that will look like!

THE MILLENNIAL KINGDOM

There are different opinions about what the Millennial Reign looks like. What other reasons do you believe make it dangerous to deny an actual Millennium?

____

____

____

____

PROPHECIES ABOUT THE MESSIAH AND THE SECOND COMING

Many believe the Second Coming of Christ is the Rapture. This is inaccurate. During the Rapture, Jesus will meet His Church in the air, and at the Second Coming, His feet will touch the earth and remain for His 1,000-year reign.

BINDING OF SATAN

The devil will be bound, along with his fellow evil companions, and chained for 1,000 years. For thousands of years, he has corrupted, destroyed, deceived, and killed countless people. What do you think he and his minions are feeling during this time of being chained in the bottomless pit?

EZEKIEL'S TEMPLE

FOCUS POINT

The temple of the Lord will be built in Jerusalem, the same location where previous temples were constructed. This shows that God has been the same yesterday, today, and tomorrow. He longs to dwell with His people. A new temple will make this possible during the Millennial Reign. Not only will Jesus reside on earth, but the glory of God will also. When He speaks, His Voice will sound like many waters. How can one even imagine what that means? The sounds of many waters. Will it be intense? Will it bring peace? The thought of it brings wonder and eager expectation. Not only will His presence reside in the temple, but His glory will fill the whole earth. We have seen glimpses of His glory; however, not to the level it will reach at that time. What are you looking forward to during the Millennium?

THE ROLE OF THE LEVITICAL PRIESTS FROM THE LINE OF ZADOK

Those with natural bodies will need to understand everything Jesus did for them. They will be taught by the sons of Zadok. The difference between those who hear the gospel during that time and those who hear it during the Tribulation is that there will be no evil at work. They will be able to make decisions based on what they learn and will not be deceived during the 1,000 years. It won't be until the very end that they will face the devil and all he has to offer.

ANIMAL SACRIFICES REINSTATED AS A REMINDER OF WHAT JESUS DID

Jesus was the final sacrifice to redeem humanity from the grip of sin and death. Similar to Communion, the sacrifices during that time will be a remembrance of what Jesus did. What are your thoughts on the fact that animal sacrifices will begin during the Millennial Reign?

1,000 YEARS RULING AND REIGNING FROM JERUSALEM

First Corinthians 15:26 says, *"The last enemy that will be destroyed is death."* This verse reveals that death is an enemy of God. Is this a new understanding for you? If so, what are your thoughts on the revelation that death is the final enemy Jesus will put under His feet?

____

____

____

____

____

____

WILL KING DAVID RULE WITH JESUS?

King David was one of the greatest kings in the Bible. He is known as "a man after God's own heart" (*see* 1 Samuel 13:14 and Acts 13:22). Even in his failures, God knew David's heart was pure and that he desired the things of God. Because of this, he will rule under Jesus and reign alongside Him. What we do here and now will prepare us for that time. Know this: even if you make mistakes, God looks to the heart. He's the forgiving God, and if you repent, He can and will use you during the Millennial Reign. Thank God for forgiveness!

GLORIFIED SAINTS WILL RULE WITH JESUS

Sowing today brings rewards during the Millennial Reign. We saw at the Bema Seat that our works will go through the fire. What remains are those things that can endure fire's heat and purification, while the others will burn away. What does sowing and reaping mean to you in eternity?

____

____

____

____

____

____

SOWING AND REAPING TODAY BRINGS ETERNAL REWARDS

After reading Luke 19:12-27, how does this process show sowing and reaping? What can you learn from this passage?

AUTHORITY GRANTED OVER TERRITORY

Luke 16:10 says, *"He who is faithful in what is least is faithful also in much; and he who is unjust in what is least is unjust also in much."* The parables of the minas and talents reveal the truth of Luke 16:10. When someone is faithful with little, they will be faithful with much. This is evident in today's financial system. Have you known someone who started with very little, yet the Lord supernaturally blessed them, changing their financial state? This will be true during the Millennial Reign. How we live now, being faithful with what we are given, will reflect how we are used during the Millennium.

KINGS AND PRIESTS

Like the Zadok priests and King David, we will work alongside Jesus. We will bear the title of kings and priests. How does this affect you and your thinking, knowing that you will be considered a king and priest at that time?

MORTALS AND IMMORTALS COEXISTING

The idea that mortals will continue to sin is mind-boggling. The devil's absence doesn't change the fact that humankind has free will to choose between right and wrong. Given that the "sin nature" will still be present during the Millennium, why do you think people will still deny Jesus?

____

____

____

____

____

____

____

UNIVERSAL KNOWLEDGE OF GOD

People will have an inner knowing of God. They will have to decide whether to accept Christ or not. The priests will teach them about Jesus, and they will also be able to see and experience Him. Imagine a world without the devil, with Jesus walking the earth and accessible to all. Those born at that time will not fully understand how amazing it is to have Jesus in the flesh. Sadly, many during that time will still choose to deny Christ and follow the devil at the end of the Millennium.

WORSHIP WILL BE PART OF LIFE

Worship is a major part of the believer's life and will continue for 1,000 years. How has worship impacted your life today?

____

____

____

____

____

____

____

THOSE WHO REFUSE TO WORSHIP

Drought is the consequence of refusing to worship. Why would anyone not want to join other believers in worshiping God? This is quite confusing. Those who don't go will face immediate drought. This shows very localized rainfall. One house and property can receive the Lord's blessing through rain, while the very next house can be dry and barren. People would know the choice of that person. The "why" question is very valid, and hopefully, many will choose to worship.

WHAT DOES LIFE IN THE MILLENNIUM LOOK LIKE?

When Jesus is finally ruling and reigning in Jerusalem, He will be filled with joy. This understanding can be deeply moving. Jesus will finally experience joy because that moment has finally arrived. How does that understanding affect you?

____

____

____

____

____

____

PEACE AMONG THE ANIMALS

As stated in previous chapters, humanity's actions have brought and will continue to bring destruction to animals. During the Millennial Reign, animals will experience a different reality. At that time, peace will be evident among them. They won't be dangerous. Given this, what experiences with animals are you looking forward to?

____

____

____

____

____

____

SATAN RELEASED AT THE END OF THE MILLENNIUM

At the release of the devil at the end of the Millennium, many will choose to follow him. There may be billions of people born during that time who will experience evil for the first time. The devil's cunning will reveal itself to these people, and they will have a choice to believe him or to choose Christ. Why do you think people will be so easily influenced to deny Christ and choose the devil?

____

____

____

____

____

____

GOD HIMSELF FIGHTS THE FINAL BATTLE FOR ALL ETERNITY!

In the final battle, God will step in and put an end to all evil. His wrath was evident during the Tribulation. However, this goes beyond wrath; it's the grand finale. When Father God steps in, that's it. There's no surviving that one. This is why it's so important to choose Jesus!

THE FINAL JUDGMENT OF THE GREAT WHITE THRONE

PERSONAL REFLECTIONS

At the very end of it all, before eternity with God and Jesus, all evil will come to know their eternal fate. The lake of fire is the final destination for Satan, hell, and everyone who allowed themselves to be deceived and to deny Christ. It's a sad reality that they will face this torment forever and ever. A question that has been asked throughout the years is, "How can a loving God send people to hell?" The answer is that He isn't sending anyone to hell; they are willfully choosing their eternal fate. Another question to ask is, "How could people choose to deny a loving God who sent His one and only Son to die and make a way of salvation?" This salvation not only saves from hell but offers so much more, as seen in the words *soteria* and *sozo*. At this point in the book, you may have learned many things you didn't know before. With these things in mind, how would you answer the first question if someone asked you that today? How has this new understanding of future events helped you know how to minister to the lost? Write down your answers.

CHAPTER SIXTEEN

ETERNITY INCOMING: FOREVER AFTER THE END

SCRIPTURES

1. **Second Corinthians 12:2-4**—*I know a man in Christ who fourteen years ago—whether in the body I do not know, or whether out of the body I do not know, God knows—such a one was caught up to the third heaven.* [3] *And I know such a man—whether in the body or out of the body I do not know, God knows—*[4] *how he was caught up into Paradise and heard inexpressible words, which it is not lawful for a man to utter.*

2. **First Corinthians 2:9-10**—*But as it is written: "Eye has not seen, nor ear heard, nor have entered into the heart of man the things which God has prepared for those who love Him."* [10] *But God has revealed them to us through His Spirit. For the Spirit searches all things, yes, the deep things of God.*

3. **Revelation 21:1**—*Now I saw a new heaven and a new earth, for the first heaven and the first earth had passed away. Also there was no more sea.*

4. **Revelation 21:2-4**—*Then I, John, saw the holy city, New Jerusalem, coming down out of heaven from God, prepared as a bride adorned for her husband.* [3] *And I heard a loud voice from heaven saying, "Behold, the tabernacle of God is with men, and He will dwell with them, and they shall be His people. God Himself will be with them and be their God.* [4] *And God will wipe away every tear from their eyes; there shall be no more death, nor sorrow, nor crying. There shall be no more pain, for the former things have passed away."*

5. **Revelation 21:5-6**—*Then He who sat on the throne said, "Behold, I make all things new." And He said to me, "Write, for these words are true and faithful."* [6] *And He said to me,*

"It is done! I am the Alpha and the Omega, the Beginning and the End. I will give of the fountain of the water of life freely to him who thirsts."

6. **John 19:30—***So when Jesus had received the sour wine, He said, "It is finished!" And bowing His head, He gave up His spirit.*

7. **Revelation 21:7-11**—*He who overcomes shall inherit all things, and I will be his God and he shall be My son.* [8] *But the cowardly, unbelieving, abominable, murderers, sexually immoral, sorcerers, idolaters, and all liars shall have their part in the lake which burns with fire and brimstone, which is the second death.* [9] *Then one of the seven angels who had the seven bowls filled with the seven last plagues came to me and talked with me, saying, "Come, I will show you the bride, the Lamb's wife."* [10] *And he carried me away in the Spirit to a great and high mountain, and showed me the great city, the holy Jerusalem, descending out of heaven from God,* [11] *having the glory of God. Her light was like a most precious stone, like a jasper stone, clear as crystal.*

8. **Revelation 21:12-21**—*Also she had a great and high wall with twelve gates, and twelve angels at the gates, and names written on them, which are the names of the twelve tribes of the children of Israel:* [13] *three gates on the east, three gates on the north, three gates on the south, and three gates on the west.* [14] *Now the wall of the city had twelve foundations, and on them were the names of the twelve apostles of the Lamb.* [15] *And he who talked with me had a gold reed to measure the city, its gates, and its wall.* [16] *The city is laid out as a square; its length is as great as its breadth. And he measured the city with the reed: twelve thousand furlongs. Its length, breadth, and height are equal.* [17] *Then he measured its wall: one hundred and forty-four cubits, according to the measure of a man, that is, of an angel.* [18] *The construction of its wall was of jasper; and the city was pure gold, like clear glass.* [19] *The foundations of the wall of the city were adorned with all kinds of precious stones: the first foundation was jasper, the second sapphire, the third chalcedony, the fourth emerald,* [20] *the fifth sardonyx, the sixth sardius, the seventh chrysolite, the eighth beryl, the ninth topaz, the tenth chrysoprase, the eleventh jacinth, and the twelfth amethyst.* [21] *The twelve gates were twelve pearls: each individual gate was of one pearl. And the street of the city was pure gold, like transparent glass.*

9. **Revelation 21:22-27**—*But I saw no temple in it, for the Lord God Almighty and the Lamb are its temple.* [23] *The city had no need of the sun or of the moon to shine in it, for the glory of God illuminated it. The Lamb is its light.* [24] *And the nations of those who are saved shall walk in its light, and the kings of the earth bring their glory and honor into it.* [25] *Its gates shall not be shut at all by day (there shall be no night there).* [26] *And they shall bring the glory and the honor of the nations into it.* [27] *But there shall by no means enter it anything*

that defiles, or causes an abomination or a lie, but only those who are written in the Lamb's Book of Life.

10. **Revelation 22:13-14**—*"I am the Alpha and the Omega, the Beginning and the End, the First and the Last."* [14] *Blessed are those who do His commandments, that they may have the right to the tree of life, and may enter through the gates into the city.*

11. **Revelation 22:3-5**—*And* ***there shall be no more curse****, but the throne of God and of the Lamb shall be in it, and His servants shall serve Him.* [4] *They shall see His face, and His name shall be on their foreheads.* [5] *There shall be no night there:* ***They need no lamp nor light of the sun, for the Lord God gives them light. And they shall reign forever and ever****.*

12. **Proverbs 8:22-31**—*The LORD possessed me at the beginning of His way, before His works of old.* [23] *I have been established from everlasting, from the beginning, before there was ever an earth.* [24] *When there were no depths I was brought forth, when there were no fountains abounding with water.* [25] *Before the mountains were settled, before the hills, I was brought forth;* [26] *while as yet He had not made the earth or the fields, or the primal dust of the world.* [27] *When He prepared the heavens, I was there, when He drew a circle on the face of the deep,* [28] *when He established the clouds above, when He strengthened the fountains of the deep,* [29] *when He assigned to the sea its limit, so that the waters would not transgress His command, when He marked out the foundations of the earth,* [30] *then I was beside Him as a master craftsman; and I was daily His delight, rejoicing always before Him,* [31] *rejoicing in His inhabited world, and my delight was with the sons of men.*

13. **Romans 4:17**—*(As it is written, "I have made you a father of many nations") in the presence of Him whom he believed—God, who gives life to the dead and calls those things which do not exist as though they did.*

14. **Proverbs 8**—*Due to the length of the text, please read from your Bible.*

15. **Revelation 22:5**—*There shall be no night there: They need no lamp nor light of the sun, for the Lord God gives them light. And they shall reign forever and ever.*

16. **Revelation 5:10**—*And have made us kings and priests to our God; and we shall reign on the earth.*

17. **Psalm 45:16**—*Instead of Your fathers shall be Your sons, whom You shall make princes in all the earth.*

18. **Psalm 149:5-9**—*Let **the saints be joyful in glory**; let them sing aloud on their beds. [6] Let the high praises of God be in their mouth, and a two-edged sword in their hand, [7] to **execute vengeance on the nations, and punishments on the peoples**; [8] to bind their kings with chains, and their nobles with fetters of iron; [9] to execute on them the written judgment—this honor have all His saints. Praise the LORD!*

19. **Isaiah 60:12-14**—*For the nation and kingdom which will not serve you shall perish, and those nations shall be utterly ruined. [13] "The glory of Lebanon shall come to you, the cypress, the pine, and the box tree together, to beautify the place of My sanctuary; and I will make the place of My feet glorious. [14] Also the sons of those who afflicted you shall come bowing to you, and all those who despised you shall fall prostrate at the soles of your feet; and they shall call you The City of the LORD, Zion of the Holy One of Israel."*

20. **Daniel 7:18**—*But the saints of the Most High shall receive the kingdom, and possess the kingdom forever, even forever and ever.*

21. **Daniel 7:22**—*Until the Ancient of Days came, and a judgment was made in favor of the saints of the Most High, and the time came for the saints to possess the kingdom.*

22. **Second Timothy 2:11-12**—*This is a faithful saying: For if we died with Him, we shall also live with Him. [12] If we endure, we shall also reign with Him. If we deny Him, He also will deny us.*

23. **Revelation 2:26-27**—*And he who overcomes, and keeps My works until the end, to him I will give power over the nations— [27] "He shall rule them with a rod of iron; They shall be dashed to pieces like the potter's vessels"—as I also have received from My Father.*

24. **Revelation 3:21**—*To him who overcomes I will grant to sit with Me on My throne, as I also overcame and sat down with My Father on His throne.*

25. **Revelation 5:10**—*And have made us kings and priests to our God; and we shall reign on the earth.*

26. **Daniel 12:13**—*But you, go your way till the end; for you shall rest, and will arise to your inheritance at the end of the days.*

27. **Psalm 48:14**—*For this is God, our God forever and ever; He will be our guide even to death.*

28. **Psalm 17:15**—*As for me, I will see Your face in righteousness; I shall be satisfied when I awake in Your likeness.*

29. **Psalm 102:12**—*But You, O LORD, shall endure forever, and the remembrance of Your name to all generations.*

30. **Revelation 22:12-13**—*And behold, I am coming quickly, and My reward is with Me, to give to every one according to his work.* [13] *I am the Alpha and the Omega, the Beginning and the End, the First and the Last.*

Understanding forever can be difficult to grasp. We live in a world of time. Everything is timed. We are told how many hours of sleep are needed for health. School and work are scheduled, and doctor's visits are timed. We live and breathe by time. There are even technologies that track how long you walk, how long you spend on your phone, and your sleep patterns. Nothing in our lives is exempt from time. Because of this, it is hard to imagine a life without the clock to worry about. Thinking about a forever scenario can be hard to wrap the mind around.

THE NOTION THAT AFTER DEATH IS NOTHING

Those who believe there is no life after death truly believe in nothing. What they don't understand is that eternal blackness is still something. What are your thoughts on the concept of nothing?

____

____

____

____

____

THOSE WHO HAVE HAD A NEAR-DEATH EXPERIENCE AND VISITED HEAVEN

Many have had near-death experiences and have returned, sharing what happened. Some have gone to heaven, while others have gone to hell. The messages they bring back can be sources of hope and eye-opening reminders to encourage people to turn from their sins and accept Christ as Savior, or else face an eternity in hell. Have you heard stories like this? What was the message they shared?

____

____

HEAVEN IS NOT THE FINAL DESTINATION FOR BELIEVERS!

Believers from every generation who have passed from this life into the next are in heaven. When the Rapture occurs, every believer will be taken to heaven while the Tribulation unfolds. After the Millennial Reign, a New Heaven and Earth will be created, and we will reside on the New Earth.

WHAT IS FOREVER?

FOCUS POINT

In a forever scenario, we will need bodies that will not fade away. Since death will be defeated, our bodies will go on without diminishing. This is why we receive new, glorious bodies that will take us through eternity. There will be no more pain, wrinkles, arthritis, or aging. We will truly be forever young. With this in mind, what part of forever are you looking forward to?

GOD IS MULTIDIMENSIONAL BECAUSE HE CREATED IT ALL!

God sees the beginning and the end at the same time. He knows what lies ahead in eternity. Earth is so small compared to everything else out there. Is it safe to say that God could have plans for the whole universe, not just the tiny planet we live on? What are your thoughts on that? Do you think God could use us for this grand plan to develop beyond earth? Write down your thoughts.

NO EYE HAS SEEN, NOR EAR HEARD

It's difficult to process the idea that there are things coming that we have not seen. This is the opposite of what Ecclesiastes 1:9 says, that there is nothing new under the sun. That verse speaks to our time on the present earth. However, this will not be the case in the end. There are things we've never imagined, dreamed of, or seen. Our minds can't create what lies ahead. This will be the biggest surprise we will ever receive. How do you think it will be when God presents us with the things He has prepared and waited so long to give to us?

A NEW HEAVEN AND A NEW EARTH ARE ONLY A GLIMPSE INTO ETERNITY FUTURE

The New Earth will have no more seas. Each landmass will be connected to the next. There will be no more division among the nations. It will be one massive nation and people. We will be the ones who endured to the end, and our inheritance is not only Jesus and eternity with our Father but also unity with our fellow brethren. Have you ever thought about that part of eternity? Unity with the body of believers? How does this minister to you today, knowing that there is so much disunity in the body of Christ?

THE HOLY CITY—THE NEW JERUSALEM

God, our Father, will walk with us on the New Earth. He will reside in the New Jerusalem. Before that time, it was known that no man could see God's face and live, yet at that time, He will be with us. After all the wars, trials, tribulations, struggles, and torments, God will wipe away every tear. How does this make you feel, knowing that everything you have ever gone through, all the hurts and betrayals, will be met with God taking His hand to comfort you, and from that moment on, you will face none of those emotions ever again?

IT IS DONE!

In John 4:13-14, it says, "Jesus answered and said to her, 'Whoever drinks of this water will thirst again, [14] but whoever drinks of the water that I shall give him will never thirst. But the water that I shall give him will become in him a fountain of water springing up into everlasting life.'" The water that Jesus spoke of mirrors the water of life that God gives us in eternity (*see* Revelation 21:6). Jesus offers us water while we are alive on earth. Jesus said we will never thirst again. What does this water represent to you now, and how are you drinking of it?

____

____

____

____

____

____

OVERCOMERS WILL RESIDE WITH GOD

For those who do not choose Christ, they will inherit an eternity separated from God and will be tormented day and night. Not only will they face the torment of the lake of fire, but their choice could be an even greater torture as they replay every moment they had an opportunity to choose Christ and denied Him instead. The absence of all that God offers can also be a form of eternal punishment, because they will know only what is the opposite of the fruits of the Spirit. This includes fear, rage, hatred, and so much more. What a sad reality for those who will inherit that. On this side of eternity, let's continue to reach a million for a billion and far beyond those numbers.

THE HOLY CITY AND THE GLORY OF GOD

The purity of God's presence will be so radiant that it will illuminate the city. There will be no need for lights because He is light. On earth, we are the light of the world. What does this mean to you, and how are you shining your light for those around you?

____

____

____

____

THE TWELVE GATES AND THE CITIES' MEASUREMENTS

Looking at the items God used to build the city shows that God enjoys beauty. What things are you eager to see and experience in the great city of God?

THE ALPHA AND OMEGA

As previously stated, the concept of forever can be incomprehensible. This includes knowing God as the Alpha and Omega. He has been and forever will be. He has seen everything, every person, location, and action, whether good or bad. Yet this doesn't change who He is. He has remained the same, with the same plan, culminating in a grand finale when every believer will walk into eternity future, side by side with the Creator Himself. There are no words to describe what that moment will feel like for Him and for us.

OPERATING IN ETERNITY FUTURE WITH THE CURSE ABOLISHED, MEANS ANYTHING IS POSSIBLE!

Of all that we will never experience again once we arrive at this eternal kingdom, what will you be happy to never face again?

TRAVEL AT THE SPEED OF THOUGHT

Since there will be no time, it only makes sense that we will be able to travel at the speed of thought. What are your thoughts on this subject?

JESUS CREATED THE WORLD AT GOD'S DIRECTION BECAUSE WE WILL BE LIKE HIM. WILL WE BE ALLOWED TO BUILD THINGS?

God has used humanity to fill the earth and subdue it. He equipped us with the ability to build and create, with the skills to transform a few items into a masterpiece. If God never changes, could He use us and the skills He placed in us to continue building and developing throughout eternity future? Please share your thoughts on this.

HUMAN BEINGS DESIRE TO EXPLORE THE COSMOS— IT IS A REMNANT DESIRE FROM ADAM'S ORIGINAL MARCHING ORDERS TO TAKE DOMINION OVER CREATION

Humanity has long been fascinated with space and exploration, always wanting to know what's out there. Why do you believe this desire is intriguing to humanity?

GOD HAS A DIVINE PLAN FOR EVEN IN DEATH AND BEYOND

For many, death is scary. There are so many questions about what happens the moment someone takes their last breath. The thief on the cross next to Jesus was told, *"Today, you will be with Me in paradise"* (*see* Luke 23:43). This shows that those who choose Christ will be with Him that same day or moment. We don't have to be afraid of dying. If you have made Jesus Lord of your life, you will close your eyes on this side of eternity and awaken to the face of Jesus. What a joyous day that will be.

JESUS IS COMING SOON!

PERSONAL REFLECTIONS

Thank you for taking this journey and for using this study manual as a tool to go deeper. *The Prophetic Endgame* and this accompanying study manual have revealed new things to me and, I believe, have opened your mind to things you never knew before. Looking back on all that you have read, those quiet times with Jesus, and the answers you have written.

For this final Personal Reflection, what has been the most life-changing information you have read? What will you take away from these two books to help you in your walk with Jesus and in how you influence those around you? Remember, Jesus is coming soon. He needs you now to reach as many as you can for Him. Let's bring God what He doesn't have—souls. Let's make God rich by bringing Him those who were lost but can be found.

Thank you once again. We love you and pray a blessing over you. In Jesus' name, amen.

NOTES

CHAPTER ONE

1. https://www.gotquestions.org/avenger-of-blood.html.

CHAPTER TWO

1. https://www.physicsclassroom.com/class/newtlaws/lesson-4/newton-s-third-law.

CHAPTER FIVE

1. https://www.biblestudytools.com/commentaries/gills-exposition-of-the-bible/luke-1-17.html.

CHAPTER SEVEN

1. https://www.merriam-webster.com/dictionary/masquerade.

CHAPTER TEN

1. https://en.wikipedia.org/wiki/Ignorance.

CHAPTER ELEVEN

1. https://nickcady.org/2020/02/18/the-statistical-probability-of-jesus-fulfilling-the-messianic-prophecies/.

CHAPTER THIRTEEN

1. https://tm.substack.com/p/sat-vocab-prevail.
2. https://biblehub.com/greek/4991.htm.

About Joseph Z

Joseph Z is a Bible teacher, author, broadcaster, and international prophetic voice. Before the age of nine, he began encountering the Voice of God through dreams and visions. This resulted in a journey that has led him to dedicate his life to preaching the gospel and teaching the Bible, often followed by prophetic ministry.

For nearly three decades, Joseph planted churches, founded Bible schools, preached stadium events, and held schools of the prophets around the world. Joseph and his wife, Heather, ministered together for 15 years and decided in 2012 to start Z Ministries, a media- and conference-based ministry. During this time, they traveled across the United States, taking a studio team with them and broadcasting live from a new location several times a week.

A season came when Heather became very ill due to hereditary kidney failure. After three years of dialysis and several miracles, she received a miracle kidney transplant. Joseph and Heather decided to stop everything; they laid everything down and ministered to their family for nearly three years.

In 2017, Joseph had an encounter with the Lord and received the word to "go live every weekday morning"—Monday through Friday. What started with him, Heather, and a small group of viewers has turned into a large and faithful online broadcast family. Today, his live broadcasts reach millions every month with the gospel and current events, which he has labeled "prophetic journalism." He additionally interviews some of the leading voices in the church, government, and culture.

He and Heather have two adult children who faithfully work alongside them. Joseph's favorite saying when ending letters, books, or written articles is, "For Jesus." As "For the testimony of Jesus is the spirit of prophecy" (*see* Revelation 19:10).

Joseph spends his time with his family, writing books, broadcasting, and training others in the Word of God.

Z MINISTRIES
BUILDING LIVES BY THE VOICE OF GOD

Joseph and Heather have ministered together for over 20 years; with a passion to see others be all they are called to be. For many years, Joseph & Heather have had the heart to offer life-changing materials and teaching at no cost to the body of Christ. Today, they have made that a reality by offering various media resources and biblical training free of charge. Joseph and Heather currently reside in Colorado Springs, CO with their two children, Alison and Daniel.

Learn more at
www.josephz.com

For Further Information

If you would like prayer or further
information about Joseph Z Ministries,
please call our offices at

(719) 257-8050
or visit JosephZ.com/contact

Visit JosephZ.com for additional materials.

Harrison House

Equipping Believers to Walk in the Abundant Life
John 10:10b

Connect with us for fresh content and news about forthcoming books from your favorite authors...

Facebook @ **HarrisonHousePublishers**

Instagram @ **HarrisonHousePublishing**

www.harrisonhouse.com